A Woman's Call

A Woman's Call

LIVING A LIFE OF PURPOSE

Evelyn Johnson-Taylor Ph.D.

TATE PUBLISHING
AND ENTERPRISES, LLC

Published by Tate Publishing & Enterprises, LLC
127 E. Trade Center Terrace | Mustang, Oklahoma 73064 USA
1.888.361.9473 | www.tatepublishing.com

Tate Publishing is committed to excellence in the publishing industry. The company reflects the philosophy established by the founders, based on Psalm 68:11,
"The Lord gave the word and great was the company of those who published it."

Book design copyright © 2013 by Tate Publishing, LLC. All rights reserved.
Cover design by Jomar Ouano
Interior design by Jomel Pepito

Published in the United States of America

ISBN: 978-1-62510-398-7
1. Religion / Christian Life / Inspirational
2. Religion / Christian Life / Spiritual Growth
13.09.06

Dedication

This book is dedicated to all the women who are diligently chasing after God. To all the women who want to fulfill the call of God for their lives. To all the women who desire to live a life of purpose, understanding that God has a plan for their lives. If you fall in any of the above categories, I dedicate this book to you. It is my sincere desire to encourage women to accomplish everything that God has designed them to do. Women, we have a place in the body of Christ, and it is our responsibility to prepare ourselves to rise up and achieve what has already been spoken over our lives.

"'For I know the plans I have for you,' declares the Lord, 'plans to prosper you and not to harm you, plans to give you hope and a future.'" (Jeremiah 29:11).

What has God said about you? What has God promised you? What is His plan for your life? This is the book for you. Woman of God, there is a call to women in these last days. Are you ready to obey the Word of God and function within your calling? As you read this book, allow the Holy Spirit to speak to you and direct you as you seek the Father for direction concerning His plan and purpose for your life. My prayer is that God may bless you always.

—Evelyn Johnson-Taylor Ph.D.

Table of Contents

Foreword

Thoughtful, insightful and powerful! Such is the writing of Dr. Evelyn Johnson-Taylor. From the very first page, you will find yourself deeply engaged in the profound truths that Dr. Johnson-Taylor brings to light. Rooted in biblical truth, each chapter, each topic compels the reader to examine him or herself in light of what God is calling us to be, calling us to do, calling us to live.

Dr. Johnson-Taylor's newest work, *A Woman's Call*, delves even deeper into the issues of "calling," both recognizing and actualizing God's call on each of our lives. Although it specifically targets women, anyone who is serious about understanding God's call on his or her life will find this *tour de force*. The reader will find him or herself thoroughly engaged by and immersed in this superb treatise. This should come as no surprise to those who have followed Dr. Johnson-Taylor's writing. Her previous works, *Women of Promise, Seven Blessing Blockers*, and *Identity Crisis*, were equally compelling. It is no wonder considering Dr. Johnson-Taylor's penchant for clarity and prayerful interpretation. Bravo, Dr. Johnson-Taylor! You have called us to our utmost for His glory!

—Alford H. Ottley, Ph.D.
Vice President for Academic Affairs
Somerset Christian College
Newark, NJ

Introduction

"For I know the plans I have for you,' declares
the Lord, 'plans to prosper you and not to harm
you, plans to give you hope and a future'"

(Jeremiah 29:11)

A written document was carried from Jerusalem
to the Jewish remnant in Babylon. Jeremiah
reminded the exiled community that ultimately it was
God, not Nebuchadnezzar, who had caused them to be
carried into captivity to Babylon.

The prophet Jeremiah had told the people of Judah
that they would experience seventy years of Babylonian
exile. In the interim Jeremiah encouraged the people to
settle in and carry on their regular day-to-day activities.
Those in exile were instructed to seek and pray for the

peace of Babylon and the other area where they were exiled. As a result of their prayers they themselves would live in peace and be recipients of God's kind sovereignty over the nations. (Jeremiah 29:5-7).

Oftentimes the calling and promises of God in our lives will not be immediate; there will be a time of preparation. There will be a time of spiritual development as well as emotional maturing. During the period of waiting, know that God has not forgotten you.

In Jeremiah 29:11 the Lord places great importance on His unalterable plan to bring calm and not affliction. God had not ended His relationship with Judah; He remembered His agreement and His guarantee of restoration.

May I say to you today, God has not terminated His plan for you. Anyone who trusts the Lord Jesus can live a life of purpose and fulfill their God-designed destiny. Any born-again woman who refuses to obey what God has called her to do is without excuse. God has a plan for each of our lives, and it is His great delight to reveal His will to all who seek Him. When believers truly purpose in their heart to seek God and devote quality time to prayer and study, God will reveal His plan for their lives. There is no great mystery to what God has designed each of us to do. The answer is found in our obedience to the Word of God.

God has a plan for each of our lives, but many people live their entire lives never fulfilling God's plan. Many times individuals will look at others and become consumed by what everyone else is doing. When a person starts to focus on others, what is visible many times is the part of that individual's life that they want you to see. I want to challenge you today to stop looking at other people. Living a life of contentment and purpose is about you and God and what He has called you to do. What God has destined for you to do can only be accomplished through your yielding in obedience to His will.

Woman of God, you are equipped to fulfill the plan of God for your life. Whatever season you may be in right now, take comfort. Seasons change, and nothing last forever, good or bad. There maybe some struggles, some hurts, and some disappointments along the way. Fear may enter your heart in your endeavor to fulfill your purpose. Do not be afraid, have faith, trust and rely on God. When one is afraid, one must look to what the Word of God brings out concerning God's total and complete love. The love of God toward His people will cast out all fear. When fear is removed, there is nothing to hinder one's faith. What He has promised, He will perform.

I say to you today, as the Prophet Jeremiah said in Jeremiah 29:11, wherever you are in life and whatever you may be facing, God still has a plan for your life. He has not changed His mind concerning you. You can rest assured that the plan that God has for you is good, it is not evil. You can hold to the anchor of hope and be confident that God will not give up on you. Even if you have made life-altering mistakes, God has not altered His plan concerning you. He stands ready and willing to finish what He has initiated in you.

Just as the Prophet spoke to those in exile, I speak to you: continue with your normal daily activities. Remain prayerful as you seek God's plan for your life. As you pray, God will reveal His plan to you. Be attentive and listen for His voice. When God speaks, do not be afraid to act.

God may choose to speak to you through your spiritual leader, through a trusted friend, or through the pages of this book. Friend, the plan God has for you can only be seen clearly when you see it through the eyes of faith as you yield in obedience to the Word of God. One can never walk in the fullness of what God has planned without first yielding in obedience.

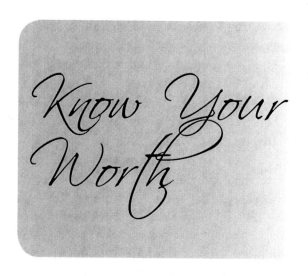

Know Your Worth

If a believer is to passionately pursue her destiny, the believer must recognize her value. Many times the message of worth is delivered and received. The hearer is excited, but the excitement soon vanishes. In our hearts we know that we are valuable, but our mannerisms do not demonstrate what we know.

Year after year women seek out conferences and retreats trying to find their purpose. They come with expectancy and excitement. No doubt many have gathered their hard-earned money just to attend, some knowing that the money they spent to get there should have been used for something else. But their hope is that if they can just make it to the conference, there, God will have a word for them.

Many women will travel from conference to conference seeking to hear from God. I am convinced that another conference is not what is needed. What is needed is an understanding and acceptance of the Word of God. In the conferences the message is preached; the tapes, books, and shirts are sold. But when the conference is over, many revert back to the same negative way of thinking. After the hype of the conference is over and all those who attended have gone back to their individual homes, what now? The cheers have stopped, but the tears continue. They are still longing and seeking for purpose, seeking for value and worth.

During my time as a ministry leader, I have encountered countless women with stories of longing and desperation. As I travel speaking to women, many of them are just seeking purpose. What is it that God has called me to do? The plan of God for one's life is not as difficult to comprehend as one might think. As one walks in obedience to God's Word, God will reveal Himself. As God reveals Himself, it is important to have a sense of value, to know who you are in Christ. Know who God created you to be. If I do not understand my value, then when God reveals His purpose I will not be able to grasp the vision of where He is taking me.

Matthew 13:44-46: "The kingdom of heaven is like treasure hidden in a field. When a man found it, he hid it again, and then in his joy went and sold all he had and bought that field. Again, the kingdom of heaven is like a merchant looking for fine pearls. When he found one of great value, he went away and sold everything he had and bought it." This parable has to do with the kingdom of heaven. Matthew 13 consists of seven parables. The first one is the parable of the sower and sets the stage as it deals with how a person hears the Word of God. There is more to hearing than what goes in the ear. The disciples do not comprehend the meaning of the parables, so Jesus has to explain it to them. He goes on to tell the parable of the tares, mustard seed, and yeast. All of these parables have to do with Christ's developing, gathering, and growing of the kingdom of heaven. During Jesus' private time with the disciples, He explained the parables. He teaches that He is the sower of the good seeds, the field is the world, the good seeds are the sons of the kingdom, and the tares are the sons of the evil one. The enemy sowed the tares. The enemy that Jesus speaks of is the devil. How many times has the plan of God been spoken over your life and the enemy came to discourage, deceive, and disturb you?

Jesus moves on to the parable of the hidden treasure and the pearl of great price. The kingdom of heaven is like a treasure hidden in the field. This parable concerns kingdom values and kingdom responsibilities. In the parable of the hidden treasure a man stumbles on a treasure trove, which he makes a determination to acquire. The second man in the parable of the pearl of great price found his treasure by carefully searching for it. Both men sold what they had in order to acquire what they found. The message of this parable is the colossal significance of the kingdom and what it means to be a part of the kingdom. To enter the kingdom one must accept and do God's will. To accept it one may have to give up certain goals and desires, which are very precious, and to abandon certain practices of life.

It is worth walking away from everything to accept and to do the will of God. It does not matter whether the discovery was the outcome of an instant or the outcome of a lifetime's search. However a person learns the will of God for their life, it is worth leaving all to wholeheartedly receive it. The kingdom of heaven is valuable, and Jesus has invited us to be a part of His kingdom, which means we are valuable to Him.

Christ pursues us because we are important to Him. He has valued mankind from the very beginning. In Genesis after God had completed His work of creation, He saw all that He had made and beheld that it was very good.

God values His creation and sees mankind to be of critical value. His nature is *agape*, and when an individual really understands her value, setbacks will not cause her to give up. An individual who understands how important she is will not lose the fight by walking in fear. When a woman knows her value, then she knows that she can do all things through Christ who gives her strength (Philippians 4:13). A woman who understands her value will not be afraid to move into purpose because with Christ all things are possible. When I know who I am, then I know where my help comes from, and I will not hesitate when God says move. It is very important to know your value. This is essential to fulfilling the call of God for your life. Once I understand who I am, then my goals become obtainable. When I understand that I belong to God, I know that my Heavenly Father is able to cause me to abound in all that I put my hand to accomplish for His glory. If I do not understand my value, then I am reluctant to pursue any of my dreams because I already see myself as less than who I was created to be. And if I see myself as less than, I do not set goals for myself because I believe that I am unable to obtain them. It really is a vicious cycle. My hopelessness causes me to live a life demonstrating what I am feeling. That is why it is so important that deliverance takes place and the cycle is broken in the lives of those who profess to love the Lord. My prayer is that this be the generation that breaks the generational curse of low self-esteem in the lives of women all over the world.

Why does God place so much value on His people? One reason is because He knows the potential of those He created. God has deposited dreams in you because He knew you would produce large interest on His deposit. As people of God it is time to begin to activate the dream on the inside. Day after day, we wait for a miracle. We wait for something remarkable to happen. But may I submit to you that you are the miracle. You are the remarkable; God wants to use you as you make yourself available to Him.

In order to activate the dream, we have to see ourselves as God sees us. God has given you what you need to fulfill His plan and purpose for your life. Just as a baby girl is born with her reproductive system in place, you already have what you need for whatever God has called you to do. As the little girl's reproductive system needs to mature and develop, so does the believer. Mother will feed, teach, and train her daughter how to take care of and preserve her body. And when she has come of age and the time is right within the covenant of marriage, the daughter will use what she has had all along to give birth to children of her own. How awesome is our God to give us whatever we need to fulfill the call He has for our lives. As the believer grows and develops into a mature walk with God, then she too can begin to walk in what God has called her to do. If you have been nourished in the Word, eating a steady diet of God's Word, then you are ready to begin walking toward your destiny, taking territory for the kingdom. When God's people understand their value in the kingdom, nothing can hinder God's plan for their lives. Women of God, now is the time to pursue with passion your purpose so that you can become everything that God created you to be.

Acceptance of what you're worth is an act of faith. Faith means that an individual chooses to trust and rely strictly on the Word of God. If God said it then I trust what He said. It is a choice I must make continuously to trust what God has said concerning me. Will you choose to believe what God has said, or will you base your vision on what your circumstances look like? Circumstances and emotions change, but the Word of God will not change. What God has said about you will remain.

There have been many times in my life I have had to remind myself of the words that have been spoken over my life. Sometimes the situation does not look like what God said about me. But I have to remain focused and stand firm on the Word of God, knowing that God is able to do whatever He said He would do. God does not lie. If God said you will, then you will. If God said you will have, then you will have. If God said you will be, then you will be. Never let anyone or anything persuade you to deny what God has said concerning you.

In the parable in Matthew 13:45, Jesus speaks of a pearl. A pearl is a very special jewel. There is not much to a pearl. If you crush a pearl, it becomes lime, ordinary chalk. What makes a pearl so valuable is not what it looks like but the all-encompassing process it must go through to come into existence.

A pearl is not carved or cut like a diamond or a ruby. If you cut a pearl, it becomes worthless. The pearl is created in the heart of a living oyster. In the murkiness of the sea, an irritant, such as a grain of sand, is introduced inside the shell. The irritant begins to cut and dig into the inner tissues of the oyster, and it then begins to secrete a substance called mother of pearl. Layer upon layer is formed around the grain of sand until it is a beautiful pearl. The oyster slowly coats the foreign body until it loses its harsh contours and becomes smooth and circular. This process is what makes the pearl valuable.

Pearls come in various colors; in some ancient cultures white pearls were associated with purity and innocence. Black and gold pearls were associated with success, prosperity, and wisdom. Pearls with a rose-colored hue were commonly a symbol of a strong and passionate heart.

Pearls with a silver luster were associated with dignity, self-control, and patience. Color does not greatly affect the price of the pearl. God created humans in different colors and sizes. These things do not have emotional impact on the value of His creation.

What does impact the life of a believer is the choices one makes. The choices that people make have a significant impact on whether God bestows blessings or consequences. Remember, God cannot lie, so if He said you reap what you sow, then that means some of the things we have sown will not bring us blessings. In Galatians 6:7 Paul writes, "Do not be deceived: God cannot be mocked. A man reaps what he sows."

Paul writes about the principle of sowing and reaping. As believers we should not fake or pretend about things concerning God. If a believer thinks he can sow to the flesh and escape the harvest of devastation, he is wrong. Now this does not mean that eternal life is earned through works but that eternal life is given to those who follow the guidance of the Spirit (Romans 6:22). The summation of what Paul writes here is that it pays to be obedient to the Word of the Lord. God can forgive us if we mess up, and I'm thankful He does. But many of the situations believers find themselves in are a culmination of things they have sown. If it took some time for your harvest to produce, it will take some time to pluck down and replant. Many believers want to hear the quick fix message. Yes, God can deliver you "just like that," but many times there are long range issues that have to be dealt with. But remember, any challenges that believers face in this life can be used in the maturing process. It is in that stage of pressing and maturing that our value increases. As one matures in the Word, greater is the impact that individual can have in the kingdom. The challenges, trials, struggles, and setbacks that one faces in life are used to grow believers in the faith. If a believer truly desires to be used by God, one must avail oneself to God's classroom of instruction. Show me a Christian who has never experienced adversity, and I will show you a weak Christian. It is through the misfortunes of life that we mature.

In James 1:3, the author writes, "The testing of your faith produces perseverance." The aim of the testing of one's faith is not to destroy the individual but to mature the individual. It is vital to every believer's walk that she learns how to endure. The only way to learn endurance, unfortunately, is to experience challenges. Hebrews 12:6 teaches us that God chastens those He loves. "Because the Lord disciplines the one he loves, and he chastens everyone he accepts as his son." God disciplines or corrects those He loves. How much does God love you? How valuable are you to Him? Have you been tried lately so that patience can be produced in you?

When we look at the value of something, it can depend on whose hands something is in. When a believer allows God to take control of her life, that believer in the hands of the Master just became more

A Woman's Call

valuable than a believer living a life of disobedience. Yes, I said it, there are those who have received Jesus as Savior and yet remain disobedient. Without Him I am nothing, but with Him, I can do all things. Let God work on you; as the Father does His work and you yield in obedience you will become more valuable to the kingdom.

How impactful are you in the kingdom? Does the enemy shake when he sees you coming? God created us. That alone makes us valuable, but when we mature and develop as we seek to follow His plan and purpose, our value increases. Do not sell yourself short. You can be everything God has called you to be and accomplish everything God has designed for you to achieve.

What has God called you to do? Whatever you believe God has called you to do, it is time to walk in your calling. Do not let another moment go by without you stepping out in obedience to do what God has called you to do. We are living in the last days, and our time is short. Busy yourself with kingdom affairs.

Women, we have an awesome responsibility in the kingdom. We have been called by God to turn this generation to Him. Our little sons and daughters are depending on us to lead them. What direction will we steer them? Will we lead them to a life of obedience to God, or will we leave them wandering aimless?

When we understand our worth and know who we are in Christ, then we can do what we have been called to do. Women, we have been called. It is time to move into position and do what God has called us to do. Allow Jesus to be the center of your life, and He

24

will surely reveal His plan for your life. You do not have to wander aimlessly through life. Our Father desires to reveal more of Himself to you each day. As you humble yourself in obedience to the call of the Father, you can fulfill the call of God for your life. Romans 12:3: "For I say, through the grace given unto me, to every man that is among you, not to think of himself more highly than he ought to think; but to think soberly, according as God hath dealt to every man the measure of faith" (kjv). God has given each of us gifts that can be used in His service. These gifts are not of our own spirituality, but God gives them so that His body can be strengthened. So what has God called you to do?

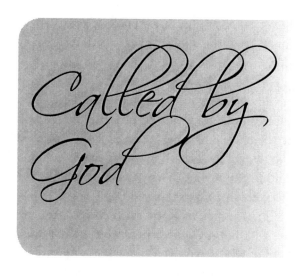

Called by God

While having the awesome privilege to grow up in the church, I often heard the Scripture "many are called but few are chosen," not really having a clear understanding of what being called meant because I had heard this Scripture for different occasions.

"For many are called, but few are chosen" (Matthew 22:14, KJV).

This Scripture was often used when an individual would come forth to openly announce their call to ministry, what is more commonly referred to as *called to preach.*

In Matthew 22:14, the word *called* in Greek, *klētos* (Strong's Concordance G2822), speaks of being invited or being called by the gospel to salvation. It does not refer to being called to a ministry office or position.

In context with the subject of this scripture, many had been invited to the wedding feast, but only a few would accept. All of Israel had been invited to follow Jesus, but only a few would consent and follow Him. We see clearly today that not all of those invited will be among the chosen of God because all will not heed the call. Many will be focused on other things and will not respond to the invitation to salvation, just like the guests who were invited to the wedding feast.

Apostle Paul writes in Romans 8: 28-29, "And we know that in all things God works for the good of those who love him, who have been *called* according to his purpose. For those God foreknew he also predestined to be conformed to the image of his Son, that he might be the firstborn among many brothers and sisters." Here the same Greek word, *klētos*, is used. In context with the subject of this portion of Paul's letter to the saints at Rome, *called* as used in verse 28 refers to those who have been invited to salvation through Jesus Christ by the preaching of the gospel. In 2 Thessalonians 2:13-14, Paul writes it out in a way that gives total clarity to the call of salvation. "But we ought always to thank God for you, brothers and sisters loved by the Lord, because God chose you as firstfruits to be saved through the sanctifying work of the Spirit and through belief in the truth. He called you to this through our gospel that you might share in the glory of our Lord Jesus Christ."

Those who are the called by God are called according to God's purpose and plan that He has for their lives. Everything that God does, He does it in order to accomplish His overall plan. He calls us to salvation to accomplish His plan, as humankind cannot fulfill God's plan apart from a relationship with Him. Second Peter 1:10-11 encourages those in the faith, "Therefore, my brothers and sisters, make every effort to confirm your calling and election. For if you do these things, you will never stumble and you will receive a rich welcome into the eternal kingdom of our Lord and Savior Jesus Christ." Peter urges the people to use their energy to confirm their calling. Without God's grace and His mercy we could do nothing and could expect nothing. But that does not release us from every possible effort. God has called us by His mercy and His grace, but at the same time we have to make every effort to move forward in the call.

Peter writes that if we accept the call to salvation and walk in it, we shall in the end receive eternal life. Peter does not mean that we will never sin. If we set out on this journey, the effort will be great, but God's help will also be abundant, and in spite of all the labor, He will enable us to keep going until we reach our journey's end.

Paul teaches in Ephesians 4:1, "As a prisoner for the Lord, then, I urge you to live a life worthy of the calling you have received." The person who has accepted God's call should live a life that equals the excellence of the calling.

Yes, all have been called, but apart from the call to salvation, what else have we been called to do? We will look at the gifts that God gives to those who have accepted the call to salvation and the offices that God calls believers to, later in the book.

When God calls an individual to function in ministry, there must be a time of preparation.

Isaiah 6:8: "Then I heard the voice of the Lord saying, 'Whom shall I send? And who will go for us?' And I said, 'Here am I. Send me!'"

Here the Lord uses the pronoun *us*. Who will go for us? *Us* refers to the Lord and His angels. Isaiah heard God saying, "Who will go for Us?" God asked a question: "Who will go for Us? And Isaiah answered God's question, "Here am I. Send me!" Interestingly enough, God asked a question, but rest assured He already knew the answer. How awesome is that when an individual hears the call being made and that person responds, "Here am I. Send me."

When Isaiah was first confronted with the vision, he realized that he was under judgment and that he was unclean and not fit to serve as a spokesman for God. In Isaiah 6:5 Isaiah said, "Woe is me! for I am undone; because I am a man of unclean lips, and I dwell in the midst of a people of unclean lips" (KJV). The seraphim touched Isaiah's mouth with a live coal and said, "this has touched thy lips; and your wickedness is taken away, and your sin dismissed."

Believers should be willing to serve God in whatever area of service is needed. God gave His Son Jesus to die for the sins of mankind. This sacrificial offering to the world should cause believers everywhere to respond in obedience to God's call. It is our gratitude that motivates us to acquiesce to the call of God.

But remember, preparation is necessary. A relationship with the Lord Jesus Christ comes first. Isaiah realized preparation was necessary.

How does one hear the call of God? Whether one hears God's call or does not hear His call depends on the condition of one's heart. An individual must have a heart that is open to hear and respond to the call of God. Many may be called, but all will not be chosen, for all will not believe and accept the invitation.

Yes, few demonstrate that they are the chosen ones. The chosen ones are those who accept the invitation to come into a right relationship with God through Jesus Christ. A right relationship with Jesus Christ will position an individual so that one can hear and respond when God summons one to a higher level of service.

The choice to respond to the invitation to salvation is left to the individual, just as the choice to respond to the call of God for service is left to the individual. Isaiah responded when he heard the voice of God. God does not force His will on mankind. Isaiah was in the presence of God, and he heard the call. His response came from a place of love and gratitude for God, and Isaiah responded in complete freedom, "Here am I! Send me."

The call of God will not be God forcing you or begging you. When Jesus called the disciples, He did it without appealing. He just said, "Follow Me." "'Come, follow me,' Jesus said, 'and I will send you out to fish for people'" (Matthew 4:19).

In order to discover God's specific plan for one's life, that individual must have a personal relationship with Christ. God's prerequisite to living the abundant life is that He must be the center of life. When an individual allows the Holy Spirit to bring one face-to-face with God, that person will hear what Isaiah heard. Isaiah heard the voice of the Lord. As one yields to the working of the Holy Spirit in one's life, that individual can say as Isaiah said, "Here am I! Send me."

God calls every person who is saved solely through the gospel. God extends the offer of salvation to all. That is why He gave His Son to die for the sins of mankind. "Who wants all people to be saved and to come to a knowledge of the truth" (1 Timothy 2:4).

When one has received Jesus by faith, what else is it that God is calling His servants to do? Remember, we have been called to fulfill God's purpose. So what is God's plan and purpose for mankind as individuals? As one begins to walk in the plan of God for one's life there will be many challenges to face. It is many times through the distress and the frustration that one comes to realize just how much God is needed in one's life. If God's plan is ever going to be accomplished in the life of His children, God must be the focus. Everything must revolve around God and His purpose.

In 1 Kings 19:1-21, Ahab reported to Jezebel that Elijah had killed the prophets of Baal. This news did not cause Jezebel to be remorseful. She instead sent word that she intended to kill the prophet Elijah. Jezebel gave authorization for Elijah to be put to death. In verse 3 of 1 Kings 19 the Scripture records that Elijah "arose and ran for his life."

After having such a marvelous mountaintop experience with God and then having killed the prophets with the sword, Elijah is exhausted. He is sick and tired of the fight. He is disappointed that nothing has changed. As he lies down in the desert under the shade of a tree, Elijah envisions facing this trial and resolves it would be better to die. He tells God basically, "I have had enough." One of the interesting things about this Scripture is how God speaks to Elijah. When Christians today envision the voice of God, many times they imagine the voice of God to be thunderous. In the Scripture, Elijah is depressed. He thought that he was alone in his commitment to God. So God visits Elijah. God is not in the windstorm. God is not in the earthquake. God is not in the fire. But God comes to Elijah in a small, still voice to let him know that his work is far from over.

I am persuaded that the reason God does not act in dramatic ways is because nothing is dramatic to Him. Nothing catches Him off guard or by surprise. And we know according to Scripture that nothing is too hard for Him. What we believe to be life-or-death situations are everyday occurrences for God.

He is not the earthquake or the tornado or the fire. He is in the gentle, still voice ready to give you instructions for your way out or for your next move.

Christians must learn to be sensitive to the voice of God. Elijah wraps his face in a cloak for this intimate talk with God. God whispers to Elijah that He is not alone. There are seven thousand others in Israel who have not bowed to Baal. God is going to provide helpers in Elijah's ministry.

Just as God provided help for Elijah's ministry, He has positioned people to help His servants today. When believers get discouraged, that is not the time to become lethargic and stagger in their own disappointment. But as children of God, we must know that God is still working in our lives. He still has a plan and a purpose for each of our lives. Even if it looks gloomy and seems like hope is lost, God has not forgotten His plan concerning those who love and trust Him.

Do not let any hindrance that you face mislead you into rationalizing that you are essential. God's purpose will be accomplished whether you do what you are supposed to or not. God will always find someone to use to accomplish His plans.

I remember many years ago when God called me to serve as a women's ministry leader. My first response was to ask God what I had to offer. The Lord showed me that He could use me if I was willing to submit to Him. It was not about me or what I had to offer, but it was about God's purpose and plan for my life.

I clearly heard the Lord say; "I desire to use you. This is my plan and purpose for you." I quickly understood that my primary responsibility was to yield to the call of God and allow Him to accomplish His task. It was that day I surrendered my body, soul, and mind to the plan and purpose that God had for my life. Yes, there have been challenges along the way, but God has been and continues to be faithful. It is a day-by-day faith walk, trusting and believing that the plan that God has for my life will be fulfilled as I yield in obedience to His Word.

When believers commit themselves in obedience to God, it is amazing how He will use them. Those who walk in obedience to the will and purpose of God are truly never alone. There are always people who have experienced the same thing that you are experiencing at that moment of opposition. Never think that you are the only one on this earth that is frustrated as you seek to fulfill the call of God for your life. Ecclesiastes 1:9: "What has been will be again, what has been done will be done again; there is nothing new under the sun."

Be encouraged, woman of God, because God is still using you and still wants to finish what He started in you. Remain obedient, and God will help you to finish strong. Paul teaches us in Philippians 1:6, "And I am sure that God, who began the good work within you, will continue His work until it is finally finished on that day when Christ Jesus comes back again."

Who does God call to fulfill His purpose? The short answer is whomever He wants to call! God has no respective person. Anyone who yields and makes themselves available, God can use. The Bible is filled, Old and New Testament, with what many could consider unlikely candidates who could be used by God. Yet we see how God used each of them to accomplish His plan and His purpose.

Living a life of obedience to God is necessary if one is to be used by God. When the people of God position themselves to be used, God will use each of them. God has great plans for each individual who yields in obedience to Him. He desires to show Himself faithful as believers seek Him in prayers.

God does not want His will to be a mystery to anyone. It is His desire that those He has called will fulfill their destiny. He wants His creations to walk in purpose and do everything He has called them to do. Do not be afraid to say yes to the Lord. God is not out to hurt you or make your life miserable, but He desires to fulfill His purpose through you. God is not trying to punish those who love and trust Him. His plans toward us are good and not evil.

God intended for His people to work together in order to do His will. He has already placed the necessary people in the necessary positions to mentor you. Some will act as encouragers, while others will challenge you. The challenges may appear to be roadblocks, but take another look: they are stepping stones to your destiny. Know that God will use every situation of your life to move you toward His plan for you.

God is interested in the particulars of the lives of His children. He is concerned about the minutiae of your life and mine. It is so important that we hear His voice and respond the first time He calls. Ignoring the voice of God can lead to unnecessary complications. Disobedience will take many down the needless path of hardship and anguish.

God has to strip down some believers before they will cry out to Him in submission. In Scripture this is evident in Jonah's plight. Do not get distracted by life's encounters, stay focused on God, and keep your ears tuned to His will for your life. When a believer is continually seeking the face of God, He will reveal Himself.

Be ready and open to whatever the Lord requires from you. Be sensitive to the move of the Holy Spirit and how God uses those around you. You may receive a message from God from the Sunday morning message, from midweek services, or from the lady next door. Your task is to be listening for His voice. Who God chooses to use to deliver His message should not matter. It is the message from God that should be received and acted upon. He may speak to you in a still, small voice. You have to pay attention, or you may miss God's next assignment for your life.

The book of Jonah is his own description of his unwise conduct and his ultimate proclamation of coming to terms with the divine call of God for his life.

Jonah felt that God would be compassionate only toward the elect of Israel since these were the people He had chosen. Many times people miss the call of God because He is calling them into an area or direction that they have no interest in pursuing. But remember it is not about you, but it is about God and how He wants to use you.

People would have no problem saying yes to the call of God if it was something they already wanted to do. The call of God will challenge you in areas where you are not comfortable. But God never calls you to do something that He will not help you accomplish. He will open the doors that need to be opened, and He will close the ones that need to be closed. The call of God will push you beyond your own security. The call of God will often stretch the believer. Those who seek to fulfill God's purpose for their lives must be willing to trust Him to do what needs to be done.

Those called by God must be willing to look beyond their own needs and desires and ask God, "What is it You have for me to do?" The self-serving person makes the mistake of rejoicing only in their own deliverance when God answers their prayer. This individual will miss out on God's plan for their own life by narrowing the grace of God. Jonah had no desire to share in God's plan to save the city of Nineveh.

When the word of the Lord came to Jonah to go to Nineveh, he fled to Tarshish from the presence of the Lord. But God had called Jonah, and He was not going to let him off that easy. God sent a mighty storm on the sea so that the ship that Jonah was on was about to be destroyed.

The sailors became afraid; they began to cry out to their gods. They began to throw cargo overboard to lighten the load, thinking that would make a difference. Jonah was in the lower part of the ship asleep. The captain came to Jonah to wake him up. "Arise and call on your God," said the captain. They also began to cast lots to see which passenger was the target of God's anger, and the lot fell on Jonah.

Jonah confessed that he was running from his call. How many times do we hear individuals say, "When God called me, I ran." God is everywhere, so let's just agree right now that you cannot outrun God. David said it this way in Psalm 139:7-12, "Where can I go from your Spirit? Where can I flee from your presence? If I go up to the heavens, you are there; if I make my bed in the depths, you are there. If I rise on the wings of the dawn, if I settle on the far side of the sea, even there your hand will guide me; your right hand will hold me fast. If I say, 'Surely the darkness will hide me and the light become night around me,' even the darkness will not be dark to you; the night will shine like the day, for darkness is as light to you."

Jonah, like David, finally realized that there was no place he could go to escape the presence of the Lord. Jonah, like many people today, was a reluctant messenger. Jonah was headed to Tarshish, which may have been the southeast coast of Spain. Tarshish represented the farthest place known to the people of ancient Israel. It would be what we would call today, the ends of the earth. The message so prevalent in the story of Jonah is that God accomplishes His work regardless of the resistance of an unwilling messenger. If God is calling you, surrender now. God wants to use you, too.

How fascinating that many today still try to run from God. Many times a person will do terrible things because they know God is calling them. The individual feels that if they are bad enough then God will not want to use them. Those are the people that God seeks out. He chastens those He loves. God will not give up on you just because you are unwilling to obey. There is no place geographically that one can go to escape the call of God. Many will make things more difficult for themselves by attempting to escape the call of God.

Precious time that could have been used for God to fulfill His purpose has been lost. God's plan lies adrift for your life when you do not heed to the voice of God. No matter what you have done, God will use you when you come to Him with a heart of repentance and obedience.

Apostle Paul killed Christians. That would seem to be the most terrible act that one could commit. But as we read in the Scriptures, God uses Saul, whose name was later changed to Paul. He called him when he was on his way to Damascus. Saul breathed threats and murder against the disciples of the Lord. Saul went to the high priest and asked for letters from him.

The letters were documents authorizing Saul to arrest Christians in Damascus. Saul's plan was to take the followers of Jesus who had escaped to Damascus back to Jerusalem to stand trial before the Sanhedrin. There the Christians would probably face a death sentence.

In Acts 9:3-9 we learn about the call from God to Saul. He heard a voice saying "Saul, Saul, why are you persecuting me?" You may be on your way to do something wrong when God calls you. But one thing is certain, once the hand of God touches your life, your life is never the same. When God calls, He gives new direction. No one who has experienced the touch of the Lord's hand can continue going in the same direction.

Some, when God calls them, will do like Jonah and try to escape to other parts of the world, attempting to outrun God. God is calling an individual on the East Coast, so that same individual runs to the West Coast. Surprise, God is there! He calls an individual on the West Coast and that person runs to the East Coast, trying to escape the call of God. When that individual arrives on the East Coast God is there. God is everywhere. King David declared there is no place he could go to flee the hands of the Lord.

The call of God for our lives may come while we are engaged in other undertakings. Many are headed down one road, and God stops them midway and reveals His plan for their lives.

John 4:5-26 details the encounter between Jesus and the Samaritan woman. The Samaritan woman did not comprehend the spiritual message of Jesus. She was thinking only of physical water and could not understand how Jesus could provide water without a means of drawing it, especially since the well was deep.

Jesus mentioned the woman's husband, which may seem out of context in this Scripture. The question Jesus asked about her husband caused her to see herself. The insight that Jesus revealed regarding this stranger led her to assume that Jesus was a prophet. How else could He have known about her private life after they had just met?

This leads the woman to shift the conversation away from the subject of her personal life to a spiritual matter. When reading this passage of scripture in John 4 we learn that this woman's prior schedule did not include meeting Jesus at the well. This was an unplanned encounter that she had with Jesus. Many times while we are actively engaged in other activities, Jesus will lay out His plan for our lives. Always be ready and willing to listen to the voice of God. We never know when He will call.

Your life can be headed in one direction, and one encounter with Jesus will most definitely change everything. I have known many great men and women of God who give testimony that they never expected to be where they are now in life. They were headed down another professional track, and God called them. College students have turned down scholarships in order to pursue God's call. Professionals who have planned out their lives confess that God stopped them mid-career and set them on another path. Many of them have walked away from lucrative income to pursue God's call on their life. There is no better, safer, more fulfilling place to be than in the will of God.

My continuous petition to the Lord is to let my life be as one of servitude for the work of the ministry. When God calls, it is a lifelong commitment. The journey of life will demand us to do self-evaluations along the way. It has been helpful for me to examine where I am in life and where I might have been if I had said no to the call of God. I can tell you without hesitation that in spite of all of the liberties that I lack concerning my life's course, the freedom I enjoy in Jesus Christ is beyond anything I could have ever hoped for. It is true that life lived with purpose is the best life a person can live.

When God called me, I willingly accepted the call, but I did have my own ideas about how to go about fulfilling God's plan for my life. When God calls us, we must remember it is about fulfilling His purpose and not our own program. Whether one runs from the calling or desires to alter the calling, all is disobedience to the One who has called you.

In addition to the woman in John 4, the Scriptures record other women who have been used by God. Women play a huge role in Scripture; I have listed many of them at the end of this book. God used many of the women of the Bible to fulfill His purpose.

Judges chapters 4-5 speaks of a woman by the name of Deborah. She was perhaps the most well-known female prophetess. Deborah is one of the five women to be called a prophetess in the Old Testament. Some of the other prophetesses mentioned in Scripture are Miriam (Exodus 15:20), Huldah (2 Kings 22:14; 2 Chronicles 34:22), Isaiah's wife (Isaiah 8:3), and Noadiah, a false prophetess (Nehemiah 6:14).

Deborah was often found under the palm tree holding court and solving the problems of the people. She is shown in the best light of all the judges in the book. Many sought out Deborah for her decisions. She is called "A Mother of Israel." This is a title given to her as one of admiration, reverence, and prominence. Deborah also instructed Barak in a strategy for battle. Read Judges 4:9-14.

Miriam, the sister of Moses, was also a woman that the Lord used. She spoke confidently from God. Miriam took the tambourine in her hand, and all the women went after her with tambourines and with dances. This Scripture describes the Israelites' first worship service following their deliverance from the Red Sea. Exodus 15:21: "Miriam sang to them: 'Sing to the Lord, for he is highly exalted. Both horse and driver he has hurled into the sea.'"

In Romans 16:7, Paul greets two fellow apostles that he holds in high regard, Andronicus and Junia, who was a woman. Translators of the Bible over a period of time changed the name Junia to Junias, making the name appear masculine. Paul states, "Salute Andronicus and Junia, my kinsmen, and my fellow-prisoners, who are of note among the apostles, who also were in Christ before me" (KJV). *Of note among the apostles* can mean either they were well-known to the apostles, or that they were well-known as apostles. Paul writes that Andronicus and Junia were Christians before he was. Junia was a Christian woman at Rome, mentioned by Paul as one of his kinsfolk and fellow prisoners. Because there is no mention of Junia and Andronicus in the gospels or Acts, the phrase *of note among the apostles* perhaps means they were known to the apostles.

God used women in Bible history, and He continues to call women today. My personal experience of being called by God began many years ago. As I became more in tune to the voice of God and began to yield myself to the leading of the Holy Spirit, things began to happen in my life. In 1994, I sensed urgency and felt a strong tugging at my heart calling me to women's ministry. My passion and my compassion for women became evident as a young, pastor's wife. Maybe later God could use me, but at this time my focus was on teaching and training our very young daughters. I had no aspirations to reach beyond the walls of our home. My focus was to teach and train our girls so that they would develop into the young ladies that God could use for His purpose and His glory. Surely God would not want me to take time away from my family to pursue His plans for my life.

It was during this time of pondering that I noticed women from different walks of life were seeking me out for advice. Many times God will place people in your life that will be able to identify your purpose before you can. That is why it is so important that we be attentive to the request of those who God sends into our path. Always be ready to serve others. Serving is a key component to fulfilling the plan of God for your life. If you truly desire to be used by God, develop the heart of a servant. Jesus came to serve, and He uses those with like character and qualities.

Little did I know that God wanted to use me to help develop not only our daughters, but to develop other women as well. Many of the women I encountered had come from difficult pasts. Many had been in abusive relationships, bad marriages, had low self-esteem, or were involved in other areas of life that I had no experience in dealing with.

I remember saying to God, "How am I going to help them?" I had been raised in a very conservative Christian home. I had never been exposed to many things of the world. My sphere was small, and my life had been protected. I wondered, *What do I have to bring to the table?* I had heard grand testimonies of God's deliverance and felt that I had nothing to share that could help the hurting women He was bringing into my life. But what I was really doing was making excuses and making the call of God about me and what I felt most comfortable doing.

God's call to me was very clear. "It is not about your experiences, but about the power of My Word to change the lives of people." What God was saying to me was that it is My Word that brings healing, wholeness, and deliverance. I was not to dwell on my history but to trust Him to do what needed to be done in the lives of those He would place in my path.

Many are drawn to God through the testimony of others; there is no doubt about that, but we have to remember it is God that changes the hearts of people. The Word of God is what breaks bondage off the lives of people. Testimonies are good and need to be shared, but ultimately it is God that redirects the lives of people.

I started with a home Bible study where women were invited to come and bring their children with them. I was not neglecting my family in any way. I do not believe God would have been pleased if I had. God wanted me to use my life as a testimony of His great power. Part of my mission was to let young mothers and young wives see me putting God first, family second, and ministry third. That was an example that needed, and still needs, to be modeled today. Many believers do not have a clear understanding of God and ministry.

I have heard too many sad stories of those who serve in ministry losing their families in the process. There are pastors who focus on building mega ministries while their homes are falling apart. One's relationship with God has to be first, but God never intended for one's ministry to come before one's family. I am convinced that my greatest ministry is to my family. If I preach and win the masses for the kingdom and neglect the souls of my family in the process, then God will not be pleased.

In that women's Bible study many years ago, my calling was affirmed. Thank God for confirmation. Once I understood my assignment, I began to prepare myself to be used by God. I enrolled in seminary; I knew that if I was to use the Word of God to set women free, I needed to have a deeper understanding of the Word of God. Preparation is so important. Whatever you believe God has called you to do, whether it be in ministry or outside of ministry, begin to prepare yourself. If you begin preparing yourself now, when the door of opportunity opens you will be equipped to walk through it.

Trusting and relying on God will get the job done. Man cannot rely on his own abilities to fulfill God's plan and purpose for his life. Yes, one must prepare, but one must also know that God will bring the revelation of His purpose through prayer and consecration. The will of God for one's life must be the center focus, and each person must seek God for direction.

Do not get sidetracked wondering how you are going to do what God has called you to do. When God gives a vision, He will also give provision. The open door to fulfill the call of God many times comes by way of our thought processes. He places a thought in your mind and expects you to carry it out. When I speak of provision, I am not necessarily talking about finances, although that is included.

A visionary looks at everything that God has given her and how she can use what God has given to make the vision a reality. When God gives directions, one cannot sit back and wait. The individual must begin to move in what God has said. For example, when I believed God was calling me to women's ministry, I started with a home neighborhood Bible study. I made flyers and passed them out to the women I came in contact with. This was before the popularity of the Internet.

I talked to women in the grocery store, in the drugstore, at my children's school. That is what I mean by moving in what God has said. Of course I bathed each endeavor with prayer, but the key is I did something.

In Ecclesiastes 9:10, when Solomon was an old man, he said, "Whatever your hand finds to do, do it with all of your might." Apostle Paul writes in Colossians 3:23: "And whatever you do, do it heartily, as to the Lord and not to men."

Just do something; finances many times are the least of our concern. Often individuals will measure success by the amount of revenue they generate. But God is not concerned with money. He is concerned with how you are doing with the assignment He has given you. Are you sitting and waiting, or are you pursuing with passion the call of God? Do not get caught up in reaching the masses. Start with your neighbor next door and your community. In some cases, start in your own home. Reaching the masses will come later if that is what God has called you to do. When an individual begins to move in God, serving in the area where God has spoken, God will supply what is needed.

The ladies came to the home Bible study, and they told their friends, and their friends came. Now with the popularity of the Internet, I can reach more women than ever. Learn to use what you have on your way to receiving more. What's in your hand? Use whatever it is to fulfill God's plan for your life so that you can bring Him the glory He so richly deserves.

God will direct you as you seek Him. It is only through the constant guidance and help of the Holy Spirit that you will be able to carry out God's appointed plan for your life. A personal relationship with Jesus promises that the Holy Spirit will live within you, giving you direction.

When an individual does not trust Jesus as Savior and Lord, that individual will go through life guessing what God's will is for her life. Without God, you will depend on your own wisdom, and most likely you will be wrong. The Scripture teaches us to trust in the Lord and not depend on our own understanding.

When discussing purpose, it is necessary that individuals understand that purpose is more than what you do. It is who you are. What you do will assist you in fulfilling your purpose, but if for some reason you cannot do that specific thing anymore, your purpose remains intact.

In life, some may discover that a chosen occupation may be closely related to the purpose God has for them. Many occupations and callings require similar personalities, similar interests, and similar motivation. But other times a job can be just that, a job. A means to an end while you go about walking in the plan of God for your life.

Initially, I went to school to be a nurse. I worked as a registered nurse for many years. After my nursing career, I worked as a real estate salesperson, assisting home owners sell their existing homes and buy new ones. Working as a registered nurse and as a real estate salesperson were my two career paths before transitioning into full-time women's ministries. It does not matter what career you are pursuing or engaged in at this moment, God can still use you. He can take the tools of your trade and use them to promote His kingdom and to build His people. Your current position may be your prelude to pursuing the call of God for your life. Never feel as if what you are doing now will prevent God from calling you. As believers we should use our careers to bring glory to God and allow Him to use us even in the workplace to honor Him.

As you seek direction for your life regarding your part in advancing the kingdom of heaven, remember God will give you everything you need to complete your calling. Your purpose is what God created you to fulfill, and the desire to accomplish it will stay with you until you leave this earth. True gratification is only found when one is walking in the plan of God for one's life.

God does have a plan for your life. It is a good plan and not an evil plan. He wants to bring you into a place that will cause you to give Him glory. Being obedient to the plan of God for your life will bring Him glory. In the process of giving Him glory, you will find yourself fulfilling your purpose, which will bring you great contentment.

Romans 12:6-8: "We have different gifts, according to the grace given to each of us. If your gift is prophesying, then prophesy in accordance with your faith; if it is serving, then serve; if it is teaching, then teach; if it is to encourage, then give encouragement; if it is giving, then give generously; if it is to lead, do it diligently; if it is to show mercy, do it cheerfully."

The Greek word for *gifts* is *charisma* (Strong's Concordance G5486), which refers to God-given skills. *A favour with which one receives without any merit of his own.* These skills or gifts should be used to build up the body of Christ. Training and development of the gifts that God gives to believers is necessary. Whether the gifts are speaking gifts or service gifts, they all are to be developed in a way that will benefit the entire Body of Christ. These gifts are given by the power of the Holy Spirit. In Paul's writing in the New Testament, he writes about the speaking gifts, prophecy, teaching, encouragement, the word of wisdom, and the word of knowledge. The apostle also covers the service gifts, helps, mercy, faith, discernment of spirits, leadership, managing, and giving. Whether God chooses to gift an individual in the area of speaking, service, or both, please know that the gifts are just that, gifts. They have been given as a favor from God, which one receives without any merit of his own. Whatever gift God desires to demonstrate through you, know that it is given by Him and it is to be used for His glory.

Prayer

Dear Heavenly Father,

I recognize that You have called me for a purpose. I pray now in the name of Jesus that You would reveal to me Your plan and Your purpose for my life. Please do not let me walk around in darkness. It is my sincere desire to walk in the plan that You have for my life. I commit myself fully to You and to Your plan for my life. As You reveal to me what it is You have called me to do, I commit to a life of obedience in my pursuit. I pledge to live a life that is pleasing to You so that I may be able to fulfill Your call on my life.

Dear Lord, I do not want my time here on earth to be in vain. Help me to walk in Your plan for me until You come back for me. I desire to be and do everything You have called me to do. I pray now that if I have stepped away from Your plan in any way that You would reveal it to me and direct me back to the right path. I promise to make myself a student of Your Word as I seek to understand Your plan and purpose for my life.

My sincere desire is to do and say those things that bring glory and honor to You. Please guide my steps today that I will walk only where You have designed for me to walk. Tame my tongue that I will say only those things that You would have me to say. Let my life be a shining example of what it means to be a believer as I seek to please You in every area of my life. I confess that I have not always done what was pleasing in Your sight. I ask and receive Your forgiveness now in the name of Jesus. I know that You died on the cross so that I could live the abundant life. I receive the abundant life by faith. This is my prayer in Jesus' name. Amen.

Principle of Ownership

The word *ownership* refers to the legal right of an individual to possess something or someone. Traditionally today in America, we do not own people, but when a person receives Jesus as Savior and Lord, that person has given Jesus ownership over their life. What one is saying is that "I am no longer my own; I now belong to Him."

If a woman is to walk in the call of God for her life, she must realize that she is not her own. We were created for God's glory and when we realize that truth, life becomes less conflicting. Each person is a designer original, created by a loving God for His purpose and for His glory. Man was created by God, for God. Many situations can come up in life that may cause one to doubt the love of God. Chronic illness, death of loved ones, being relieved of employment, failed relationships, or anything one considers a setback can rattle one's faith. These types of struggles in life many times will cause an individual to ask questions of God.

In the Scriptures, the book of Job is about a righteous man who suffered greatly. When satan asked permission to attack Job, God granted satan's request. So if God loved Job, why did He allow satan to attack him, you might ask? Job was a wealthy man who lost everything he had. Job even lost his children at the hand of satan, and God allowed it to happen. Job 1 records that Job was blameless and upright, meaning he was an honest man. His character was impeccable, and ethically he was faultless. It is important to note that Job was righteous before his social critics but not completely sinless before God. The Bible teaches "For all have sinned and come short of the glory of God" (Romans 3:23). Job 31:5-6 reads, "If I have walked with falsehood or my foot has hurried after deceit let God weigh me in honest scales and he will know that I am blameless." Job 31: 1-40 is Job's promise of innocence and Job's invitation to God to punish him if He finds him guilty. Job wants God to judge him fairly.

The book of Job also records that Job feared God and shunned evil, which indicates that his right relationship with God encouraged him to run away from wickedness. Job's relationship with God was more important to him than to engage in wicked activities.

Job had a wife, seven sons, and three daughters. In the ancient Middle East, having a large family was considered to be a sign of God's favor. It was also viewed as a symbol of strength. Looking at the size of Job's family, this tells us that God had blessed Job. In Psalm 127:3-5 the Scripture reads, "Children are a heritage from the Lord, offspring a reward from him. Like arrows in the hands of a warrior are children born in one's youth. Blessed is the man whose quiver is full of them. They will not be put to shame when they contend with their opponents in court." Children are a heritage; they are God's gift to parents. A full quiver of children was the mark of God's blessings. When a home appeared blessed in ancient culture it gave the father a degree of honor within his community. Christians today continue to view children as a blessing from God.

On the day when the sons of God came to present themselves before the Lord, the Bible says that satan was among them. The Lord questioned satan, "from where do you come?" Now we know that God knows all things, but this was part of God's conversation with satan. So God said to satan, "have you considered my servant Job?" In Job 1, satan questioned Job's motives for fearing and serving God. Does Job have ulterior motives for serving God?

God had placed a hedge of protection around Job and his household. No harm could come to him unless the Lord gave permission. In one day Job plunged from the apex of success to the lowest of deficiency. He must have felt that God had left him.

When Job began to question God regarding his situation in Job 7:11-21, he said:

> Therefore I will not keep silent; I will speak out in the anguish of my spirit, I will complain in the bitterness of my soul. Am I the sea, or the monster of the deep, that you put me under guard? When I think my bed will comfort me and my couch will ease my complaint, even then you frighten me with dreams and terrify me with visions, so that I prefer strangling and death, rather than this body of mine. I despise my life; I would not live forever. Let me alone; my days have no meaning. "What is mankind that you make so much of them, that you give them so much attention, that you examine them every morning and test them every moment? Will you never look away from me, or let me alone even for an instant? If I have sinned, what have I done to you, you who see everything we do? Why have you made me your target? Have I become a burden to you? Why do you not pardon my offenses and forgive my sins? For I will soon lie down in the dust; you will search for me, but I will be no more.

Like Job, many times hurt and disappointed people will pour out their anguish and complaints to God. There are those who become bitter when things do not work out according to their plans. These individuals become angry with God. Notice in Job 42:7 God did not reprimand Job for questioning Him. "After the Lord had said these things to Job, he said to Eliphaz the

Temanite, "I am angry with you and your two friends, because you have not spoken the truth about me, as my servant Job has." Job revoked his own opinion, acknowledged his pride, and maintained that God's purpose for his life was supreme.

It is important that believers understand that God has made provisions for whatever misfortune befalls them in this life. Since our God is all knowing, He knows what we will encounter in this life. He knows what tragedies will befall us. We can rest in the fact that He promises to never leave us nor forsake us and that He will be with us always. *Little comfort* you might say when I am in pain and the doctors cannot tell me what is wrong. When my world is falling around me, I need to know where God is, some might say.

Life will sometimes beat you down, but your trust must remain. That is easier said than done when unemployment is at an all-time high. Families cannot pay bills and are losing their homes in seemingly affluent neighborhoods. Parents are frustrated when their children are rebellious and stay out all night. Children are being abducted from their homes, and mom and dad have no idea if they are living or dead. It is in those times when our faith is tested and many want to know where is the God who promised never to leave me?

We want to remind God of our faithfulness. We want God to remember our good deeds. Many will question God as to whether or not they deserve this, asking, "Is this some kind of a punishment? Judge me fairly, Lord. Others have lived a much worse life than I have, and all is well with them."

Friend, the question is not where is God? But the real questions are "God, do I trust you?" and "God, do I understand that I belong to you?" Solomon said, "Time and chance happen to all." Ecclesiastes 9:11. It is important to remember who we belong to and know that God wants to get the glory out of our lives.

We must learn the principle of ownership. I belong to Him. And if I belong to Him, He can do whatever He wants to do with me at any time, and He does not need my permission. When a person totally commits to God in obedience, that individual can take comfort in the fact that they belong to God and His hands are the best hands to be in. Romans 8:28: "And we know that in all things God works for the good of those who love him, who have been called according to his purpose." As believers we will not always understand the process, but we do have the assurance that God's purpose is being completed in our lives. Life's bumps may not feel good, but remember, all things work for the good of those who love God and have been called according to His purpose. It is not about my purpose and what I want to do but God's purpose. The Scripture teaches that all things work for the good for those called in agreement with God's purpose. God collaborates in all things for what is good for His children. The word *together* (Strong's Concordance G4903) in Greek is *synergeō* meaning to work together, help in work, or be partner in labor. God is the one who controls all things for our good; we must not fight against God's plan for our lives.

The principal reference of *all things* is the suffering of this present time. In Romans 8:18 Paul writes, "I consider that our present sufferings are not worth comparing with the glory that will be revealed in us." The KJV uses the word reckon instead of consider. The Greek word is *logizomai* (Strong's Concordance G3049) meaning to count, compute, calculate, and to count over. Paul came to the conclusion that the glory will outweigh any suffering that any believer has to go through. All situations will work together in aid for the believer's good. The believer will be conformed to Jesus Christ now and rule with Him later. Those who love God are those who are called by God. The believer's love is the believer's reaction to the work of the Holy Spirit in her heart. We are called according to His purpose. God does everything, including redemption, in order to achieve His complete plan for the lives of those He gave His Son to save. First Corinthians 10:13: "There hath no temptation taken you but such as is common to man: but God is faithful, who will not suffer you to be tempted above that ye are able; but will with the temptation also make a way to escape, that ye may be able to bear it." All believers have to deal with some form of temptation. But God is good in that He will not let His children endure anything for which He has not equipped them. His grace is sufficient for whatever a believer may go through in this life. Paul is writing to the Corinthians, but believers today can receive this word of comfort also. The different things that we experience are not rare. Everyone who has claimed the name of Christ has experienced some temptations.

Whatever we experience, God will give us the grace and power to endure. God may not show up in the way that we expect. He may not be in the earthquake, tornado, or fire, but know that He has not left you to suffer alone.

The fact that we belong to God allows Him to do as He likes with us. Belonging to God also means that He can use us as He desires. God desires to fulfill His plan and purpose in the lives of those who love and trust Him. The believer's responsibility is to say yes to the Lord. When believers come to the realization that they are not their own, and that they have been bought with a price, there is a shifting of the mind-set. Understanding the principle of ownership will cause believers to have a strong desire to obey the One who purchased them with His own blood. Allowing God full control over your life opens the door for His will to be done in your life and through your life. It is wearisome to fight against God's plan for your life.

When reading Job's journey, one can understand why Job had questions for God. Job wants to know what he has done to deserve such harsh punishment. How many times do believers feel as if they are the target of satan? Sometimes you may feel as if the enemy has direct access to your life. Many times it seems as if God has forgotten you, but let me assure you that God still has a plan and a purpose for your life. He has not forgotten you; Scripture teaches us that He knows us by name. Isaiah 43:1: "But now, this is what the Lord says—he who created you, Jacob, he who formed you,

Israel: "Do not fear, for I have redeemed you; I have summoned you by name; you are mine."

The Lord's use of the word *name* shows His close connection with the Israelites. He had revealed His name to the people and affirmed their name to Pharaoh. When we read Isaiah 43:1 the word *created*, translated from the Hebrew verb *bara'*, means "to fashion, to shape, to form." (always with God as subject) (Strong's Concordance H1254). The word *formed* means "to fashion, or frame of divine activity" from the Hebrew word *yatsar*, (Strong's Concordance H3335). The use of these verbs suggests that the Lord's creation of Israel as a people was as pivotal an act as His creation of human beings in the beginning.

The New Testament pronounces Christians as new creations in Christ. Second Corinthians 5:17: "Therefore, if anyone is in Christ, the new creation has come: The old has gone, the new is here." A believer's life will change because she is being changed into the likeness of Christ. God is now in control of the new believer's life. God knows what He is doing. We are His people, and He is our God.

Understand the principle of ownership. If I own something, I can do with it as I please and when I please, right? God is the authority; He has the final word concerning your life. Job feared that God would destroy him, but when God responds, He does not come to destroy Job.

Challenges in the life of a believer are not meant to destroy the believer. They are not meant to break the spirit of those who love God. Challenges come to make one stronger in the faith. Life has a way of knocking the wind out of your sails. As a ministry leader I have witnessed some who have fainted by the way. The storms and challenges of life proved too difficult. Others have struggled to hold on in the midst of the storm. As an encourager, it has been my great privilege to pray with those who are disheartened, to stand in the gap and intercede for them when they felt they could not pray. Knowing I have walked through some of the same or similar storms stands as a testimony that the same God who brought me through is available to all who seek Him.

In my endeavor to fulfill God's call on my life there have been some disenchantments that might have taken me off course. The one thing that magnifies in my mind is that God can be trusted. In the midst of the storms, God is steady. He does not move back and forth, vacillating from one decision to the other. We belong to God, and we can depend on Him always. When things seem to be sinking all around you, turn to the Scriptures. Proverbs 3:5 admonishes us, "Trust in the Lord with all your heart and lean not on your own understanding." We must not focus on what we believe or what we think, but we must focus on God and who He is in our lives. As we submit our desires to Him and follow His directions the path becomes clearer.

Yielding to God is always the best choice to make. He always has a better way than we could ever imagine. It is through the tough times that the believer can see God building her faith and strengthening her for the task ahead. Trials are never a waste; they are to be used as a time of building and maturing. When you are going through the storms of life you may want to say, "Lord I am mature enough." But understand that these afflictions are a part of your process of becoming who God has called you to be. It is the struggles that we overcome that will allow us to speak life into others that may be sinking as well.

God did answer Job in chapters 38-42 with a series of questions. God instructed Job to brace himself like a man. Not only did God have questions for Job, but God said to Job, "You shall answer me." Read the last five chapters of Job to see the list of questions God asked Job. I have listed just a few of the questions below.

> Then the LORD spoke to Job out of the storm. He said: "Who is this that obscures my plans with words without knowledge? Brace yourself like a man; I will question you, and you shall answer me. "Where were you when I laid the earth's foundation? Tell me, if you understand. Who marked off its dimensions? Surely you know!
>
> Who stretched a measuring line across it? On what were its footings set, or who laid its cornerstone—while the morning stars sang together and all the angels shouted for joy? "Who shut up the sea behind doors when it burst forth from the womb, when I made the clouds its garment and wrapped it in thick darkness, when I fixed limits for it and set its doors and bars in place, when I said, 'This far you may come and no farther; here is where your proud waves halt'? Job 38:1-11

God did not come to destroy Job, but he did give Job many things to ponder. One thing that God wanted Job to consider is, "who is in charge here?" Job had to submit to God's authority. God challenged Job in order to teach him.

The questions that God asked were designed to alert Job to the aftermaths of his grievances and demands. Friends, no matter how many questions we have about what is happening in our lives, we are no match for God. God asked Job, "Were you there when I laid the foundation of the earth?" Job, where were you? God alone commands the morning and the evening. It has nothing to do with you, my friend, but it is all about God and how He desires to do things. God does grant us some freedom, but we cannot go beyond His control. Before anything was, God was.

In Job chapter 40 Job declared his unworthiness in relation to the almighty God by placing his hand over his mouth. He realizes he is unable to give a proper response to God's questions. Again God asks Job to prepare himself like a man. God is not finished teaching Job submission. When the questions were over, Job's response was, "Surely I spoke of things I did not understand, things too wonderful for me to know" (Job 42:3). How many times do modern-day Christians feel as Job did, but after the frustration we realize that we spoke of things we did not understand. If we could see what God is doing in our lives in the midst of the trials and tribulations, we would be more patient.

Solomon writes in Ecclesiastes chapter 9, when he is now an old man looking back on his life. The things he writes about are hard lessons that he has learned along the way. Regardless of all the wisdom he possessed, he made foolish choices in his life. Solomon had many regrets; he had looked to the wrong source for happiness and joy.

One can learn a great deal from Solomon. He said in Ecclesiastes 9:1-2, "So I reflected on all this and concluded that the righteous and the wise and what they do are in God's hands, but no one knows whether love or hate awaits them. All share a common destiny— the righteous and the wicked, the good and the bad, the clean and the unclean, those who offer sacrifices and those who do not."

When one reads the book of Ecclesiastes and takes heed, it will help one to avoid the same mistakes that Solomon made. The sum of what Solomon learned is that to live without God is meaningless. God created man for His glory, and man is only fulfilled when he is performing within the guidelines for which he was created.

Isaiah 55:8: "For my thoughts are not your thoughts, neither are your ways my ways," declares the Lord. God's thoughts surpass all mortal imagination.

Ephesians 3:20: "Now to him who is able to do immeasurably more than all we ask or imagine, according to his power that is at work within us." Human beings cannot fathom the depths of God's wisdom. The limited understanding that we do have of God is only what He sees fit to reveal to us.

Truly God's thoughts are not our thoughts, and His ways are not our ways. He has a different agenda than the one we operate on. Nothing can thwart the plan that God has for you except your disobedience. Do not look at your current situation or your current circumstances; God still has a plan and a purpose for you. Sure life may not have turned out as you expected, but remember God's ways are not our ways and His thoughts are not our thoughts. Isaiah 55:8-9: "For my thoughts are not your thoughts, neither are your ways my ways," declares the Lord. As the heavens are higher than the earth, so are my ways higher than your ways and my thoughts than your thoughts."

To try to imagine what God is thinking is enough to blow a human's mind. We must have faith. Trust and rely on His Word that whatever He said will happen. While we as humans are trying to figure God out, God has already answered the request. He knows the end from the beginning. Man does not and will never know the mind of God. That is why the Scripture teaches that we must walk by faith and not by sight. Many times what we see is an illusion, perhaps a trick of the enemy to take us off course. Trust God in all that you do; He does have a plan for your life.

Life can take many unexpected turns leading us in many directions. You may look at your life and wonder, *How did I end up here?* Many things that happened to you in your life were not part of your plans. Some of them were bad things that never should have happened. But because we live in a dysfunctional society, bad things happen. Sin is prevalent every day. Innocent people are killed, and many families never get justice for crimes against loved ones. We live in a fallen world.

Jeremiah 17:9: "The heart is deceitful above all things, and desperately wicked; who can know it?" The mind, the feeling, and sometimes the actions of people are wicked. Bad things do happen to good people. However, one thing believers must always do is remain focused on God and continually strive to know His plan and purpose for their lives. Believe me, He has one for each of us. Before you were born God had a plan for you. You were not an accident, and you are not here by mistake. It was all part of God's divine plan to bring you into the world at His appointed time so that you could fulfill His divine purpose on the earth.

In order to walk in the plan and purpose of God for your life, obedience is mandatory. Obedience is not something one does when it is convenient or comfortable. As believers we must submit to a life of obedience and allow the Holy Spirit to direct each and every day of our lives. Daily submission, moment by moment, this should be the prayer of every believer. Each day requires a fresh commitment to the Lord. A renewed yielding of the will to the will of the Father is needed daily.

As human beings, it is vital that we trust God. He knows the plans He has for His creation. Mankind must come to a realization that we are mere mortals and our abilities are limited. One must come to the understanding that God is all powerful and all knowing and that human beings are not.

Each person has to recognize that they are not their own, but that they have been bought with the precious blood of Jesus. He paid the sin debt for the world and those who have accepted Him as Lord and Savior now belong to Him. There comes a reckoning moment in the life of every believer. The moment they must reconcile in their mind to follow the plan of God for their life.

Believers seeking to please the Father must totally surrender to Him. Allowing Him to take the lead is the only answer to fulfilling one's destiny. Permitting God to have full control of your life is the formula for your success. When God is in charge, He will take you places you have never dreamed of going. You will be able to accomplish things that would otherwise be impossible.

With God in the driver's seat, one's life will be rich and full. Please note that by using the word *rich*, I am not referring to monetary or material possessions. I am speaking of being fulfilled. Yielding to God will allow Him to take you places you have never been and allow you to do things you would otherwise not do. *Places* may mean geographically, or it may be levels of mental maturity, both spiritually and emotionally. His plan is full, complete, and meaningful. There may be setbacks along the way, but make the choice to see them as stepping stones. What some may call starting over simply may be a new season in your life.

We relocated to Tampa ten years ago not really knowing what was ahead. Leaving a very stable and comfortable life in Maryland, we headed south to what many of our friends referred to as starting over. I never looked at it as starting over; I saw it as a chance for new experiences. During the process of this new adventure we had to let go of some things. There were many hard adjustments that had to be made, but we were walking in what we believed God had called us to do for that season of our lives. Looking back now, I can see the doors of opportunity that God opened for me to effectively walk in my calling even during what was a difficult transitional period.

There are periods in life that God has to remove the security blanket. He must take us out of our comfort zone in order for us to see the fullness of His plan for our lives. During these times of uncertainty it is important that we remain committed to the vision that God has placed in our heart. After arriving in Tampa I did not function in ministry for a period of time. But one thing we must remember is that just because you are not functioning in your call does not mean that God has changed His mind concerning what He has called you to do. Times of rest can be good as God can use this time to replenish you for the journey ahead. Use the break to be productive, and remain diligent in prayer and study, so you will be able to hear God's voice.

First Corinthians 2:9: "However, as it is written: 'What no eye has seen, what no ear has heard, and what no human mind has conceived' the things God has prepared for those who love him." Only the Holy Spirit can reveal the truth of God's plan for the life of those who trust and surrender to Him.

Many believers get frustrated when faced with challenges. Our walk with the Lord is not an easy walk, and rest assured that trials will be a part of it.

In Romans 8:35-37, Paul writes we (born-again Christians) are more than conquerors in tribulation, distress, persecution, famine, nakedness, danger, or sword. So, clearly our circumstances do not dictate our victory over the world—our faith in Jesus does.

As it is written: "For your sake we face death all day long; we are considered as sheep to be slaughtered. No, in all these things we are more than conquerors through him who loved us. For I am convinced that neither death nor life, neither angels nor demons, neither the present nor the future, nor any powers, neither height nor depth, nor anything else in all creation, will be able to separate us from the love of God that is in Christ Jesus our Lord." Romans 8:36-39

Always remember who you belong to even in the midst of trials and trouble. It is vital that we keep our focus on the one who has called us. So when the storms come, and we know they will, we must have a clear understanding that we have been called by God. If God has called me, nothing can separate me from His love. Apostle Paul assures believers that our security in Christ is complete.

Prayer

Dear Heavenly Father

I surrender my entire being to You. I willingly submit myself to You today. Make out of me what You desire me to be. Do with me what brings glory to You. I humbly confess that I am not my own. I belong to You. I understand that the call You have for my life is centered in Your purpose. I meekly and whole-heartedly give myself to Your plan and purpose for my life. I know You have plans for me, and I bring every fiber of my body into subjection now. I surrender myself helpless before You. My will, my mind, and my emotion, I command that each part of my body conform to the direction of the Holy Spirit. My thoughts, my speech, and my reasoning I command to come under subjection. I speak God's Word over my desires that they would become Your desires in the name of Jesus. Body, I command you to come in line now, yield to whatever God has planned. I am no more my own. I have been bought with a price, and I give myself to You. Even in the midst of storms, trials, and temptation, I desire to please You. I will not be moved by confrontation, by adversity, by opposition, or any other thing that seeks to take me off course. I am Yours, Lord, every part of me, and I freely give myself to You. In any way that I have strayed, please forgive me. Many times I have wandered off the path to follow my own way, and for that I repent. There have been times when I have looked at my situation and have begun to question and doubt Your love for me. I sincerely ask that all that I do or say from this moment forward bring glory to You. Dear Lord, I understand that my security in You is sure. According to Your Word I know that nothing can stop You from loving me. In Jesus' name I pray. Amen.

As women of God, we are called to be holy women. This is our first call. Before ministry, marriage, motherhood, or anything else, God calls us to be like Him. What does it mean to be holy? Many times we think living holy is what people see when they look at us. Many believe, and have been taught, that a holy person is one who dresses conservatively or modestly. Some people believe that being holy means that "If I wear my dress below my knees, and do not wear any makeup, never smile or have any fun, that will make me holy." There are individual churches that teach holiness based on outward appearances. If I do not cut my hair and never cover my gray then I am holy. If I do not go to the movies or to the beach then I am holy. God is still calling women today to be holy, but it goes much deeper than your outer appearances.

Many are confused when it comes to living a life of holiness. What does it really mean? I can tell you with a great deal of certainty that wearing long dresses, wearing no makeup, missing good, clean movies, and avoiding the beach does not make an individual holy. You can wear your dresses dragging the floor and never put on a dab of blush and still not be holy.

There are others who believe that being holy means to act righteous while looking down on sinners. Many church people will shun other church people who do not go to the holiness church up the street. Some have said, "You are not my sister in Christ because you look different from me." Some even say if we do not attend the same kind of church then we are not brothers and sisters in Christ. This may sound ridiculous, but these are things I have heard with my own ears and seen with my own eyes. To think that one is better than another is not what is meant by being holy. The Scripture teaches in Romans 3:23, "All have sinned and fall short of the glory of God." The Word is very clear that no one can appear more righteous than another.

Isaiah 64:6: "All of us have become like one who is unclean, and all our righteous acts are like filthy rags; we all shrivel up like a leaf, and like the wind our sins sweep us away." The word *unclean* means that the people were unfit for God's presence. *A filthy rag* refers to clothes stained during menstruation making a woman unclean. *Like a leaf* implies the people's insignificance and departure from God. No one has anything to gloat about. Without God man is nothing.

In Leviticus 11:44 (KJV), the Scripture reads, "For I am the Lord your God: ye shall therefore sanctify yourselves, and ye shall be holy; for I am holy: neither shall ye defile yourselves with any manner of creeping thing that creepeth upon the earth." The Hebrew word for *holy* is *qadowsh* (Strong's Concordance H6918). This word means saint, set apart, and pure. As a noun it means God (by eminence), an angel, a saint, a sanctuary, holy (One) saint. In the Old Testament we see that there was only one way for God to dwell among men. The only way for God to dwell among man was to make man holy. Man was instructed to consecrate himself, meaning to make himself holy. Holiness is the foundation. To be holy means to be separated to God. In Leviticus and Exodus, we see the priests continually offered sacrifices for the sins of the people.

So what is holiness? Holiness is a transformation of the heart. Once the heart has been transformed, the change becomes evident on the outside. In order to be holy, one must have a relationship with the Lord. This individual must be walking in obedience to what the Word of God says.

As believers are separated to God, they become more and more conformed to the image of God. First Peter 1:16: "For it is written: 'Be holy, because I am holy.'" Women, we are called to be holy, and this is a call we must take seriously.

Therefore, with minds that are alert and fully sober, set your hope on the grace to be brought to you when Jesus Christ is revealed at his coming. As obedient children, do not conform to the evil desires you had when you lived in ignorance. But just as he who called you is holy, so be holy in all you do; for it is written: "Be holy, because I am holy."

1 Peter 1:13-16

To be holy, one must prepare one's mind for action. This is a call that requires preparation of the mind. One must prepare one's mind for the trials that will come on this Christian journey. To live a holy life will not be easy. It requires discipline and devotion. God has called His people to holiness regardless of the obstacles. Many things will come against your quest to live holy, but God has called us to holiness still.

To live a life of holiness, the need to exercise self-control and to be watchful is necessary. Those who seek a life of holiness cannot be influenced by such things as pride, greed, and lust. One must be constantly watching for the things that seek to take an individual off the course that God has planned. As a believer one must be aware that the closer one gets to God the greater enemy one becomes to satan. An intimate walk with God will anger satan and cause him to put up every hindrance that he can. Despite all the deception of the enemy, God is yet calling His people to holiness. Second Timothy 1:8-9: "So do not be ashamed of the testimony about our Lord or of me his prisoner. Rather, join with me in suffering for the gospel, by the power of God. He has saved us and called us to a holy life—not because of anything we have done but because of his own purpose and grace. This grace was given us in Christ Jesus before the beginning of time."

To be holy requires that we be bold in our faith. God is holy, and everything that refers to Him is holy. Holiness is the very essence of who He is. Our lives must exemplify who He is if we are His children. His call to us to be holy is for His own purpose. The plan of God for our lives will always line up with His own purpose. Often when people think about purpose they immediately start thinking about things they want, what they want to accomplish in life, thinking of things they can do that will bring them happiness. Living a life of purpose has little to do with your selfish desires but everything to do with what brings God glory. What is His purpose for me? How does my desire connect with God's purpose for my life? That is the real question. How can my life be used to bring glory to God?

My daughter asked me once if I could pray for her regarding something she truly desired. She felt she needed this one thing to happen in order for her to be happy. Now, I understand that she was young and when you are young your perception is somewhat blurred. I do not mean that in a negative way because we have all been there where we feel we know best what we want and need. She said, "Can you pray that I get..." I replied, "I cannot pray that prayer for you." I took the opportunity to explain to her how important it is that her life line up with God's plan. Selfishness has become all too common in our culture today. It appears to be more about what I want and less about what God's plan is for my life. This was a teachable moment for me as a mother and as a woman of God to speak into the life of my daughter. I am so thankful for these moments that God presents for us as believers to encourage those who may be young in the faith to trust God. I agreed to pray according to God's will for her life. I never want to be outside of God's will, and I certainly do not wish my children to be outside of the will of God. There is safety in His will. There is joy in His will. There is fulfillment in His will. Now I ask you, where would you rather be?

As a testimony to my daughter, God did grant her what she was seeking at the last hour. She now has a stronger understanding of what it means to pray according to the will of God. We do not know what tomorrow holds, but God does. As believers we have to make a conscious decision every day to remain under the safety that is provided by remaining obedient to the will of God. It can be so easy to seek our own way and go in our own direction. God is calling us to holiness, and this means that we have to forsake our way for the ways of holiness. We must seek the ways of God. He is holy and His ways are holy.

At times this can be a very challenging task to accomplish. It will require self-discipline, which is something nature fights against. The flesh wants what it wants now, no restraints. But self-discipline is the only way to accomplish the task to be holy. Yes, we all want to live a life full of excitement and wonder. The very nature of man seeks things that are pleasing. The Bible teaches that we were born in sin. We have a sinful flesh by nature. That is what is normal to us, to sin. But when we become a new creation in Christ, we take off the old man and put on the new man. We shed the sinful nature and put on the mind of Christ. It is a day-by-day process, taking off and putting on. Yes, your flesh says look out for yourself today, but the God in you says, "God, you know the plans that you have for me, and if I have to walk through this to get to that, then I accept it." Many times believers may have to walk alone. If that is what one has to do to be in the will of God then press on even if you have to press alone. For we know that we are never alone because He is there with us every step of the way. God promised to never leave us alone, and I find Him to be a very good companion. Life can drain you in such a way that you will feel alone even while others are around you. Walking through illness with my husband has left me feeling alone many times. Some of the conflicts that I encounter are so intimate and so personal that it becomes very difficult to express them to others. Even though you cannot share the details of your pain, God always knows. His presence is always a constant friend as one journeys through life. Whether we are on the mountain peak or in the valley, He is near to ensure that we endure.

In this life believers are faced with many unexpected challenges. Many of life's turns could be seen as an excuse to abandon the call of God for your life. Life will reveal many things that one could never anticipate, but in the end it is clear that it was God's plan all the time. Who would have ever known that when I married my husband over twenty-two years ago that a number of those years would be spent with me being his caregiver? I am convinced that it was not a coincidence that God gave my husband a registered nurse for a wife. It was God's design, seeing many years down the road what he would need. When I think of the awesomeness of God, it is so awe-inspiring. The love that God has for His people is everlasting. Even when we mess up, He still provides and orchestrates our lives in such a way that no matter what season we enter, provision is there waiting. No wonder Jeremiah declared in Lamentations 3:22-23, "Because of the Lord's great love we are not consumed, for his compassions never fail. They are new every morning; great is your faithfulness."

God remembers to be merciful and compassionate. Every season of life presents fresh challenges, but it also presents us with new opportunities to experience the mercy of God. That is why I trust Him with my entire being. I know He has a plan for my life and He knows what He is doing. He is lining up the events right now in your life that will take you to the place He has designed for you. And He is doing it in such a way that only He can get the glory. In this life we will be faced with encounters that would attempt to take us off path. But we must remain focused on who God is and who He has called us to be. The same God that called you is well able to keep you in the middle of trials, storms, temptations, and other adversities that may occur as you endeavor to be holy.

My challenge to you, woman of God, is to stay the course. God really does have plans for your life. It may appear at times that things are swinging out of control, but remember God is in control. He knows what He is doing. God really is all that and more.

God is everything His Word declares that He is, and this includes holy. To deny that He is holy is to deny who He is. When we deny who He is, we are denying God. God is able to heal, deliver, and set free. He is able to break yokes off the lives of people. He can do anything but fail. He is all sufficient. If we deny that He is able to heal, then we are denying that He is God. To deny any part of God, any portion of who His Word says He is means that we are denying God. To deny that He is able is to deny that He is who He says He is. So when life brings you hardship—and it surely will—we have to remember that God is able to deliver.

You may have lost many things that were dear to you, but God is able to restore because He is a restorer; that is who He is. Jesus replied, "What is impossible with men is possible with God" (Luke 18:27). Life may have offered you brokenness, loneliness, and pain, but remember that whatever was taken from you, God wants to restore it and make it better than before. That's just the kind of God He is. That is what He did for Job; He gave him more than he had before. The challenge for the believer is to not get caught up in complaining. To complain about the condition will cause one to remain in the broken state. God is a restorer of those who have been broken. To deny that He is a restorer is to deny that He is God because every part of who He is makes Him God.

As women called by God, our desire is to be like Him. If we desire to be like Him, then we must desire to be holy. When faced with a situation that could cause one to behave in a self-centered manner one must choose to be holy. One must make a decision to put on the mind of Christ. I must rid myself of the old thoughts, and begin to think like Christ would think. And the way I know how Christ thinks is to become a student of the Word of God. I do not just read the Word, but I put into practice what I read.

Living holy means that I live according to the standards of the Word of God. I take on the character of God. What is His character? One of His character traits is holiness. Am I saying you have to be a saint? Be divine? No, that is not what I am saying. But what I am saying is that you need to put forth every effort to be like God. After all we were created in His image. As an individual becomes more and more conformed to the image of God, that individual will become the person God intended them to be, holy.

Genesis 1:27: "So God created man in his own image, in the image of God created he him; male and female created he them" (KJV).

The word *image* in Hebrew means to resemble and to represent. It also means likeness, similitude, to model after, to shape, or to be like. When God made human beings He made them like Himself, to represent Him, to model after and to be shaped like Him. That is how He made mankind. When man fell in the garden things changed. But our God loved us so much that He sent His Son Jesus to die on the cross for our sins. Jesus died to redeem us back to the Father so that we could once again be like Him. He created man in His image, like

Him. His love for us was so great, and He desired so much for us to be like Him.

First Corinthians 6:20: "You were bought at a price. Therefore honor God with your bodies."

First Corinthians 7:23: "You were bought at a price; do not become slaves of human beings."

When looking at being bought at a price, think of the history of slavery. I remember my mother telling me about slave auctions, how people were sold like a bag of goods. Once the slave was purchased, he belonged to the one who had purchased him. The slave now had to obey the owner because the owner had paid for him. Jesus paid the price for mankind so that man could be redeemed from sin. We were slaves to sin, but thank God for the blood that Jesus shed on the cross to pay our debt. God sent His Son to buy us back. Jesus bought us back with His blood, so that we could be redeemed back to the Father, back to our original state, the way He made us, in His image. We no longer have to obey satan. We have been purchased by the blood of Jesus so we have to obey our master. He is calling us to holiness.

> When I consider your heavens, the work of your fingers, the moon and the stars, which you have set in place, what is mankind that you are mindful of them, human beings that you care for them? You have made them a little lower than the angels and crowned them with glory and honor.
>
> Psalm 8:3-5

David is in awe at the splendor of creation, the wonders of nature. Even the universe with its infinite distances is the work of the Lord's fingers. Marvelous are the works of His hands. Woman of God, you are a work of His hands. If you are a work of His hands, then that makes you marvelous. Whatever God does, He does with purpose. That fact that He created man means He has a purpose for man. The word *man* in this text refers to all human beings regardless of gender. King David is basically saying, "God, the value you place on me—well, it is almost too good to be true." Humans stand at the top of God's creation.

The word *'elohiym* was used in the original language for *angels*, and it means rulers, judges, divine ones, angels, gods (plural) or god, goddess, godlike one, works or special possessions of God, the true God (plural intensive-singular meaning). (Strong Concordances H430). So what the writer of Psalm 8 is saying is that, God, You made man a little lower than the godhead, a little lower than Yourself. "You have made him to lack little of God." Man was created to be like, to model after God. When mankind fails to be like the Creator, man is not fulfilling his true purpose.

To be holy means that I am devoted to the pursuit to be like God. It means that I desire to have the same character that God has. Holiness in the believer involves grace, righteousness, integrity, love, peace, and mercy. These are characteristics of God. Once we become His children, we are to take on the same character as our Father. As a woman of God, my desire is to resemble my father.

As holy women, we can leave a godly legacy for our children. When we live a life of obedience and submission to God, we have the ability to impact not only our natural children, but we can impact the lives of other young women whose lives God has allowed us to touch.

The Bible teaches us as women that it is our responsibility to train the younger women. In Titus 2 Paul teaches the older women that they are to behave as becoming to holiness. We are not to bear false witness, but to be teachers of good things. The older women are instructed to teach the younger women to love their husbands, to love their children, to be of sound mind and to be pure, to be clean, and to teach them what it means to be holy.

Apostle Paul also teaches in Ephesians 4:12-14 "to equip his people for works of service, so that the body of Christ may be built up until we all reach unity in the faith and in the knowledge of the Son of God and become mature, attaining to the whole measure of the fullness of Christ. Then we will no longer be infants, tossed back and forth by the waves, and blown here and there by every wind of teaching and by the cunning and craftiness of people in their deceitful scheming."

In the book of Ephesians, Paul writes about three phases. First he writes about unity in the faith and in the knowledge of the Son of God. He writes about becoming perfect and finally attaining to the whole measure of the fullness of Christ.

That word *unity* means unanimity, agreement. *Perfect* means complete furnishing, and equipping.

The word *fullness* means completeness, abundance, fulfilling, and keeping. This is not something that can be accomplished quickly. It is a process that the believer must walk through. It requires discipline on the part of the believer. Preparation is necessary to fulfilling one's destiny.

Paul teaches that we are to live as Jesus lives. We are to pattern our lives after His. God has called us to maturity. If we are to live holy, we must mature day by day. If God's purpose is to be fulfilled in our lives, we must be equipped. To live holy is a process that we walk out each and every day of our lives. In this generation of instant gratification, this can be a foreign concept. No one wants to go through the process. We want what we want right now, no waiting. Seldom do we have to wait for anything anymore. We no longer need to wait in long lines at the banks because we have automatic teller machines, or you can get cash back at your local grocery store. Most of our banking can be done from our own home online, even making deposits. Automatic bill pay makes postage stamps almost nonexistent. Life is designed to make life comfortable for everyone.

Now we can prepare our parcels to be mailed from the comfort of our home by using our computers. No more standing in long lines at the post office. Everything is quick and convenient. Things come fast and easy, not like our forefathers, who had to exercise patience in a way that we would find strange today.

In this era with all of these modern amenities people seem to be less tolerant and more impatient. Many do not want to put forth the time and effort needed to accomplish a task. For those who desire to be holy, patience is necessary.

God has called women to holiness. The pursuit of holiness is a process. Maturing as a believer does not happen overnight. Much time must be spent in prayer and Scripture reading. We must seek the face of God and yield in obedience to His Word. In the pursuit of holiness, that is what is required. In the pursuit of holiness, there will be detours along the way. It can be easy to become sidetracked by the glamour of the world. The struggle for authenticity is a continual one. One of the areas of ministry that God has called me to function in is to spiritually develop women. Sometimes it becomes tiresome that the right doors are not open for me to do what I have been called to do. When I look through the eyes of my flesh, the vision that God gave me for Women of Promise seems unattainable, but I must be holy and remain attentive to the path that God has me on. The war between the Spirit and the flesh continues, "Do I obey God and wait for His timing or do I promote myself in a way that will cause things to happen sooner?" For those who truly seek to be holy, waiting for God's perfect timing is necessary.

Apostle Paul is a good example. After his conversion, he spent time growing and maturing in the faith (Galatians 1-2). This growth process, for many, can be painful as one pursues the plan of God for one's life.

In order to live a life of holiness, one must know Christ. In Philippians 3:10-11 Paul writes: "I want to know Christ—yes, to know the power of his resurrection and participation in his sufferings, becoming like him in his death, and so, somehow, attaining to the resurrection from the dead." What is the greatest desire of a Christian? Moses says to God: "I pray you show me Your glory" (Exodus 33:18). David prays: "As the deer pants for the water brooks, so my soul pants for You, O God" (Psalm 42:1). And Paul says that his heart longs to "know Him and the power of His resurrection and the fellowship of His sufferings" (Philippians 3:10).

The greatest desire of a true Christian is to know God. Every serious born-again believer desires to live a life pleasing to God. Every other desire pales in significance to knowing Him.

When we read Paul's request in this Scripture we do not see any material request for the apostle. But what we see is the heart of a man wanting to live holy, a man longing, wanting to have an intimate relationship with Christ. Paul is saying, "I desire to know Him."

Well, you may ask, "If I am a Christian, don't I know Him?" John 14:8-9 teaches us that Phillip, after following Jesus, said, "'Lord, show us the Father and that will be enough for us.' Jesus answered: 'Don't you know me, Philip, even after I have been among you such a long time? Anyone who has seen me has seen the Father. How can you say, 'Show us the Father'?'" The word *know* comes from the Greek word *ginōskō* (Strong's Concordance G1097) to learn to know, come to know, get a knowledge of, perceive, feel, to become known, to know, understand, perceive, have knowledge of, to understand, to know, Jewish idiom for sexual intercourse between a man and a woman, to become acquainted with, to know, be resolved, be sure. When you know someone, there is a soul tie formed, a bond that is not easily broken. Knowing someone requires a level of intimacy that onlookers do not experience.

When the Bible speaks of knowing God, it is not referring to a merely intellectual exercise. Knowing God does not mean knowing facts about God. Knowing God is not just reciting the history of His life on earth or hearing testimony of what He has done in the life of another. Knowing God involves encountering Him. Knowing God means that one has spent quality time with God learning His attributes.

When I know God, I know His character. I know God is holy. Isaiah 6:3 reads, "And one cried unto another, and said, Holy, holy, is the Lord of hosts: the whole earth is full of his glory" (KJV). God is holy and He requires the same from those who profess that they belong to Him.

Knowing God means that I know what makes Him glad and I know what grieves Him. I have spent face-to-face time with God, and as a result of time spent with Him, I have come to know Him.

A face-to-face encounter is when people seek the face of God by getting on their knees before God. Christ wants to have a soul tie with His children. Our Heavenly Father wants us to know Him. He desires to form a bond with us that cannot be broken, one that is fixed and sure. The bond He desires to have with us is one that will not be broken by adversity, sickness, pain, heartache, or disappointments, the kind of bond that only grows stronger during the challenging times in our lives.

God has called each of us to a life of holiness, and there is no way to avoid it if we truly desire to please Him. He stands ready and willing to assist those who seek to please Him. The challenge has been given. Make up your mind to fulfill the call today. Start now by living holy as God has called you to do. As people seek to obey, God will direct them on the path He has designed for them to follow. As a woman of God, start to prepare yourself to be who God has called you to be so when opportunity knocks you are where God wants you. Seek to have a character that pleases God and be ready to pursue your destiny. Only you stand between purpose and fulfillment.

Prayer

Dear Heavenly Father

Your Word declares that I am to be holy because You are holy. I understand that holiness is a way of life. To be holy is not about my outward appearance, but it is about a heart committed to pleasing You. I pray now, in the name of Jesus, that You would cause me to walk in obedience to Your Word. My desire is to know You and to be like You. As I seek to be like You in every area of my life, I pray for Your guidance and direction. Each day brings new temptation and new challenges, but my heart is turned to You. Help me to keep my gaze upon You. Help me to guard my heart for out of it flows the issues of life. My cry to you today is, Lord, I want to know You. My earnest desire is to have an unbreakable bond with You.

Help me, Lord Jesus. I pray to strive each day to be more and more like You. Show me the way that You would have me to go. Reveal to me the secret desires of my heart so that I may commit them to You and line up according to Your Word. Blind my eyes to things that are not of You, I pray. Keep my heart and my mind focused on You. Do not let me stray to the left or to the right. It is my desire to remain focused on You and the plan that You have for my life at all times. My desire is to keep You at the center of my life. Nothing else matters. You are the center of my life. I confess that I am not my own, that I have been bought with the precious blood of Jesus. I realize that it was Your great love for me that caused You to give Your only Son to die for my sins. Because of the cross my sin debt was paid. I freely surrender my life to You. Take control of my life and use me as You see fit. Humbly I submit to You, and I thank You for counting me worthy to be called Your child. Help me to develop Your character in every area of my life. Your Word says that You are holy, and Your Word says that I should be holy. I confess that I cannot do this of my own strength but that I need Your help to be holy. Thank You, Heavenly Father, for Your strength on which I can depend. I boldly confess that I can do all things through Christ who makes me strong according to Philippians 4:13. In Jesus' name I pray. Amen

Single

The world we live in today is filled with activity and clamor. Noise seems to be everywhere we turn. Crowds are on every corner. No one really wants to be alone. With all the uproar and busyness of this world, when it is silent, people become uncomfortable. Have you ever walked into a silent room? Most people are not comfortable with silence. You can see this when you are having a conversation and there is a lag in the discussion. One person will quickly interject a new topic for debate.

Our society is hungry for fun and excitement. Something has to be going on twenty-four hours a day. More money is spent on entertainment than anything else. This is evident by the huge income that entertainers receive in relation to other workers.

Many times people will have the radio or television on even if they are not listening or watching. The noise makes the environment more relaxed for them. People sometimes will hang out with other people that they do not like to avoid spending time alone. There seems to be a negative component to being alone.

The Scriptures record a number of times where Jesus went away from the crowd to be alone. Matthew 14:13: "When Jesus heard what had happened, he withdrew by boat privately to a solitary place. Hearing of this, the crowds followed him on foot from the towns." John the Baptist had been beheaded, and the disciples came and took away John's body and buried it. The disciples went to tell Jesus about it, and Jesus departed to be alone. It would seem that there is something soothing about being alone. It is in the quiet moments of our lives we can hear the voice of God.

Luke 4:42: "At daybreak, Jesus went out to a solitary place. The people were looking for him and when they came to where he was, they tried to keep him from leaving them."

Mark 7:32-35: "There some people brought to him a man who was deaf and could hardly talk, and they begged Jesus to place his hand on him. After he took him aside, away from the crowd, Jesus put his fingers into the man's ears. Then he spit and touched the man's tongue. He looked up to heaven and with a deep sigh said to him, 'Ephphatha!' At this, the man's ears were opened, his tongue was loosened and he began to speak plainly." Jesus took this deaf man aside, privately, apart from the crowd to heal him.

Marvelous things can happen in one's private time. Do not be afraid to be alone. The Word of God promises that God will neither leave you nor forsake you. When Jesus Christ is the center of an individual's life, that person is never truly alone. Friends may be few, and the crowd may be thin, but Jesus promises to stick with you until the end. Hebrews 13:5: "Keep your lives free from the love of money and be content with what you have, because God has said, 'Never will I leave you; never will I forsake you.'" In the Greek this Scripture contains two double negatives similar to the saying in English. "I will never, *ever ever*, forsake you." God will not abandon you.

You may be in the season of your life where you are single. Sometimes you feel lonely and wonder if God knows that you don't like this. Well, let me assure you He knows your every thought.

His Word declares that He knows everything about our situations. "Thou knowest my downsitting and mine uprising, thou understandest my thought afar off" (Psalm 139:2). God is active to search and test His servants. If you belong to Him, then take comfort in the fact that God knows everything there is to know about you. He actually knows more about you than you know about yourself. He knows man's intentions, longings, and words before they are expressed. He knows everything there is to know about you entirely. But remember the purpose of His intimate knowledge of His servants is protective and helpful, not critical and condemning.

God desires an intimate relationship with His people. Paul writes in Philippians 3:10, "I want to know Christ—yes, to know the power of his resurrection and participation in his sufferings, becoming like him in his death." Paul was willing to reject his own righteousness in order to secure an intimate relationship with Christ. Paul sought an ongoing experience with Christ. Women, we must be willing to reject everything to draw close to God. Having a husband cannot be a priority. God must be first. What does it mean to be "called to singleness" for your life? All believers are called to love God. However, God calls some Christians to serve him in the state of sexually abstinent singleness.

For most people, being single is a season of their lives. Some, however, remain single all their lives, either by choice or by circumstance. For those who choose to remain single, you might ask why. Some people are selfish, and they want to remain free of marriage, and if that be the case for you, please know that you are doing someone a big favor by not bringing them into a self-centered relationship with you. Singleness can be a time of satisfaction and contentment. Just because an individual is single, it does not mean that person is lonely. There are many single people who live fun, fulfilling lives. There are many married people who are lonely in what would appear to be a good marriage. A person can feel isolated and secluded inside of a marriage where both parties are not focused on pleasing each other. Many Christian marriages experience loneliness. The busyness of life will cause couples to become preoccupied with things outside of the marriage, thereby leaving the marriage to suffer. Both parties have to be actively involved in order for each of them to be fulfilled in their marriage.

If I can stress anything in this chapter, it would be that marriage is not the answer to loneliness. I know too many married Christians who are lonely. They have no similar interest with their spouses. Some of them do not even enjoy each other's company. Many of them have been married for years, and when the children grow up and leave they realize how little they have in common. Many years have gone by where they existed as a couple with their main responsibility being parenting. Now that the daily parenting duties are finished, both of them find themselves lonely while in the house with each other. This can also happen early in the relationship as well. Loneliness can set in when a couple is not focused on maintaining a good relationship with each other and individually with God.

There is a place in the heart of every human being that can only be filled by God. When we begin to search outside of God for fulfillment, we end up disappointed. I believe the best reason to remain single is that being single you have fewer distractions and more time to serve God.

Apostle Paul writes in 1 Corinthians 7:32-35, "An unmarried man is concerned about the Lord's affairs—how he can please the Lord. But a married man is concerned about the affairs of this world—how he can please his wife—and his interests are divided. An unmarried woman or virgin is concerned about the Lord's affairs: Her aim is to be devoted to the

Lord in both body and spirit. But a married woman is concerned about the affairs of this world—how she can please her husband. I am saying this for your own good, not to restrict you, but that you may live in a right way in undivided devotion to the Lord." Single people are presented with excellent opportunities to devote more time to God.

I also believe the best reason to get married is that two people believe they can serve God better as a couple than alone. Marriage works best when both parties are focused on how they can please God as a couple.

Love is important in a marriage for sure. Compatibility is good, and security is desirable. But more importantly, will your marriage enhance your walk with God or hinder your relationship with Him? If it is evident prior to marriage that entering into covenant agreement with this other person will have a negative influence on your Christian walk, then it is best to remain single.

Some are called to be single while others have a strong desire to be married. I am often asked, "How do I know if I am called to be single or married." Well, my short answer is found in Psalm 37:4: "Delight yourself in the Lord, and He will give you the desires of your heart." If you have a desire to be married, then chances are you were not called to be single. That is my short answer, but really it goes deeper than that. In this chapter, I will attempt to show you through the Word of God how you can know if you were called by God to be single. My goal is that at the end of this chapter you know without a doubt God's plan for your life regarding marriage.

God said in Genesis 2:18, "And the Lord God said it is not good that the man should be alone; I will make him a help meet for him" (KJV). This is the first time a negative assessment appears in the Bible. God did not want Adam to be lonely, so He formed a helper equal to him. This Scripture indicates that this partner would be truly fitting and fully sufficient—just right. The key here is that God did not want Adam to be lonely. So if you are single and lonely, then you are probably not called to be single. God does not want you to be lonely.

If God has called you to be single, know that He is able to provide you with the strength and to sustain you in walking out His plan for your life. Just as with any other calling, you will face challenges, but know that God is faithful to fulfill every promise to you. In 1 Corinthians 7, Paul writes that if one is unmarried it is good to remain unmarried, but if one cannot exercise self-control, let him marry. In this Scripture, Apostle Paul is answering questions that were sent to him. He continues his writings by emphasizing it is better to marry and honor God than to fall into sinful lust. If you are a single, adult woman and find yourself lusting after men, you should get married. If you are a single adult who is permissive and cannot seem to maintain sexual purity, singlehood is not for you. Those who God has called to singlehood will maintain their sexual purity. It may not always be an easy task, but because this is an area God has called you to, you want to honor God with your entire being, including your body.

First Corinthians 6:19–20: "Do you not know that your bodies are temples of the Holy Spirit, who is in you, whom you have received from God? You are not your own; you were bought at a price. Therefore honor God with your bodies." Paul stresses that sexual sin is done against the body. He was encouraging the Corinthians to escape every temptation to indulge in sexual sin. Believers today have been purchased with the precious blood of Jesus. Since we belong to Him, we must honor Him with our bodies.

Knowing God's will for your life requires persistent prayer. As you seek God in prayer, He will reveal His plan for your life. Many times He reveals it gradually. As you walk in obedience to what you know is right, God will reveal more and more to you.

In Matthew 19:11-12 Jesus replied, "Not everyone can accept this word, but only those to whom it has been given. For there are eunuchs who were born that way, and there are eunuchs who have been made eunuchs by others—and there are those who choose to live like eunuchs for the sake of the kingdom of heaven. The one who can accept this should accept it."

Jesus indicates that remaining unmarried is only for a few people. Some people do not marry because they were born with no desire. There are others who do not marry because they want to give more to serving God. Those who do not marry in order to serve God have been given the gift of celibacy in order to do this. Some individuals may profess that they are waiting on God for a spouse, but in the meantime they are actively seeking for themselves. By actively seeking I mean that they are testing the waters and tasting of the forbidden fruit. When a believer is waiting on God for a spouse, that individual lives a life of chastity while they wait. There is nothing wrong with socializing, but women, we must be careful to avoid situations where our virtuous character can be compromised.

Singleness is one of those areas, like most in our lives, that requires acceptance of the grace God gives for today and each day that follows. For many, singlehood will be a temporary season of their lives; seasons of life change. One can live in obedience, acceptance, and contentment for the present season, trusting God to prepare them for other seasons as they may come. Whatever season of life you may be in, have faith in God. Continue to seek His plan and His purpose for your life. Do not sit around waiting for Mr. Right to come. It is not God's plan for you to put your life on hold while you are waiting. The waiting process can be very frustrating, as anyone who has been single can tell you. The challenge is to not let it frustrate you, but to use this season of your life to fulfill God's plan for you. Single women can add greatly to the kingdom while they are waiting.

When an airplane goes into a holding pattern, this means an airplane makes several 360° turns to avoid other aircraft or wait for a clearance to land. Reasons for an airplane to go into a holding pattern can vary. It could be because of bad weather or scheduling delays of other aircraft.

A holding pattern is not a good place to be. Nothing is accomplished; you are just waiting for the landing.

Your mind and your focus are wrapped up in what is about to happen and when it will happen. Are you going to land safely? When will you land? Why are you not landing? While in the holding pattern, the passengers' frustrations are increasing moment by moment. Many of the passengers are wondering how this delay will impact their ground connections. The point I am trying to make is if you allow yourself to go into a holding pattern while you are single, it can be frustrating. You will always wonder when the love of your life is coming. Is this the one? How much longer before I land? Go ahead and occupy yourself fulfilling the plan of God for your life. Luke 19:13: "And he called his ten servants, and delivered them ten pounds, and said unto them, Occupy till I come" (KJV). A certain nobleman told his servants to occupy till he returned. The word *occupy* here means not merely to "possess," as it often does in our language, but to "improve, to employ in business." So I do not sit idly and wait, but I pursue the call of God for my life while waiting for my mate.

Get busy serving others. Women are not created to hunt, but we are to observe and wait to be found. Proverbs 18:22 says, "Whoso findeth a wife findeth a good thing, and obtaineth favor of the Lord" (KJV). When God brought Eve to Adam, He presented her to Adam. Let God present you to your mate. Ladies, call off the hunt! Psalm 37:4 reads, "Delight yourself in the Lord and He shall give you the desires of your heart." The desires of the heart for every believer should spring forth from the Lord. What does God desire for you?

When we seek God first and His desires become our desires, God promises to fulfill our desires.

Many time ladies will settle for a man that may not be God's choice for them because they want to be married. *Strong warning: Never want anyone or anything more than you want to please God.* Do not be afraid to pursue your destiny while you wait for God's choice of a husband for you. There are many things you can do in the kingdom as a single woman. God has used women throughout Scripture, and He continues to use them today.

Some ladies will enter relationships with men because they feel like time is running out. When women reach a certain age they feel that they have to get married. They begin to say things like "It is now or never. My clock is running out if I want to have children." Stop watching the clock and keep your eyes on the one who stepped into time, creating time.

When God brought Eve to Adam in the garden, imagine Adam's delight. Eve was created to be Adam's partner in life. Marriage was instituted and ordained by God. And God has a man just for you; just as He brought Eve to Adam, He will bring you to your husband. Your Adam is seeking God for you now, but you must be patient and wait until he finds you.

I remember my husband telling me, after we were married, how during his morning run, he would pray and ask God for a wife. I did the same thing on my morning run, praying, asking God for a husband. We realize that we were most likely praying at the same time while out running, asking God for each other.

Remain focused on God's plan for your life, and in His time He will bring you together with the mate of His choice for you.

For a marriage to be successful, God has to be the center. When Adam and Eve disobeyed God, they were separated from God, and their marriage was in trouble. Adam blamed her, and she blamed the serpent. Peace and harmony were gone from the marriage.

As a single Christian woman, do not let anything or anyone come between you and your commitment to follow God's plan for your life. Any deterrence needs to be avoided. Sometimes your conscience will tell you to go for it just as the serpent told Eve in the garden. Be wise; realize that some things are not for you, at least not now.

There is much significant advancement that a single person can make in the kingdom. Do not be fooled by the enemy; do not rationalize your curiosity, but continue to put God first. When you yield to the leading of the Holy Spirit, God can use you to bring many souls into His kingdom through your testimony of chastity.

But if you are single and you feel that God has not called you to be single, you need to pray and ask God for a mate. Getting married is the easy part, but the question is "will the marriage bring glory to God?" Marriages that do not bring joy to the husband or the wife bring God no glory.

Marriage is a ministry. Marriage is more than he loves me and I love him. Marriage is more than having companionship, more than just having someone to spend time with. Marriage is coming together as one and serving one another. Marriage is you pray for me and I pray for you. When I am weak, I lean on your strength. Marriage is about watching each other's back and covering each other. When you are stressed, depressed, and disgusted, your spouse should be able to intercede for you. When you feel like you cannot hear from God, your spouse should be able to speak a Word from the Lord into your life. Marriage is having someone to help you pray through a crisis. When you fall down, your mate is there to help you get back up again. Husbands and wives need to be able to minister to each other. If you are not ready for ministerial duties, then you are not ready to get married.

Each believer should purpose in her heart to make sure her choices bring glory to God. Matthew 6:33: "But seek first the kingdom of God and His righteousness and all these things will be added to you." We have to desire God's righteous rule on this earth and over ever decision that is made. God has to be *the* priority, not *a* priority.

Do not fall into the trap of letting others make you feel bad about your status in life. As a single person you are complete in Christ, and nothing is missing. Learn to be content with whatever season of your life you are in.

Eve got into trouble when she disobeyed God in the garden. Genesis 3:4-5: "And the serpent said to the woman, you will not surely die for God knows that in the day you eat of it your eyes will be opened and you will be like God; knowing good and evil" (NKJV).

She did not know who she was. If Eve had recognized that she was already all God meant for her to be, then she would not have been persuaded by the serpent to seek more knowledge. The serpent told her "you will be wise, and your eyes will come open." Single ladies, it is important to know who you are. When you know who you are, you are less likely to be taken off course by a handsome, smooth-talking man. You have a rich inheritance; enjoy your single life. If this is God's plan for you, embrace it and seek to do only those things that bring glory and honor to Him who created you in His own image.

Psalm 37:1-7: "Do not fret because of those who are evil or be envious of those who do wrong; for like the grass they will soon wither, like green plants they will soon die away. Trust in the Lord and do good; dwell in the land and enjoy safe pasture. Take delight in the Lord, and he will give you the desires of your heart. Commit your way to the Lord; trust in him and he will do this: He will make your righteous reward shine like the dawn, your vindication like the noonday sun. Be still before the Lord and wait patiently for him; do not fret when people succeed in their ways, when they carry out their wicked schemes."

While you are single, whether it be single by choice, single by God's design, or single in waiting, do not get anxious. Patience will be needed for the journey. Learn to depend on God. Develop a sense of dependence on Him. Learn to enjoy the Lord, enjoy your singleness, which is a gift from God.

If you are single and you do not believe you have been called to singlehood, it is important to use your time wisely. Don't go into the holding pattern, but busy yourself in service to the kingdom.

While you are single and in waiting, it is always a good idea to have an accountability partner. Seek out other young ladies with the same focus as you have, other adult, single women who are serving while patiently waiting on God for their husbands. Be accountable to each other; learn to pray together; be open with each other in your communication. If you feel yourself weakening, ask the women in your group to pray with you and to hold you responsible. When either of you go out with someone of the opposite sex, let someone know where you are going. Tell someone who you are going with, and use good judgment in your decision making. Going out with another couple is never a bad idea, especially if this is someone you just met. Safeguard your commitment to God while you wait for His choice for you.

Commit your way to the Lord. Give it over to Him and rest in Him. Be still, knowing that He has a good plan for your life. To be still does not mean to be inactive; it means to actively depend on God. To be still means to be quiet and listen. It means to wait patiently for him. While you are waiting, be actively serving God and one another. Terminate the worrying, and allow God to reveal His plan for your life.

If you are still not sure if God has called you to be single, here are a few things to remember. Do not be afraid. If you desire to be married, it is never too late.

Just make sure your reasons for wanting to be married are correct. On the same note, if you think you are to remain single, make sure your decision to stay single is for the correct reasons. Some people choose to remain single out of fear. They have had a front row seat to so many disastrous marriages that they want no part in that. Remember, God has not given His children the spirit of fear. Marriage can be a wonderful thing when God is at the center. Singleness can be a real blessing when one's life is used to honor God. But married or single, it is vital that our deepest longing be for God and what He desires for our lives. Our uttermost desire must be to please God with every area of our lives. Our bodies are God's temple, and we must honor God in how we use our bodies.

Prayer for Singles

Dear Heavenly Father

I come boldly before Your throne of grace confessing Your Word over my life as a single Christian woman. I pray that You would help me to live a godly life. It is my desire to live a life that is holy, sanctified, and set apart for You. I desire to be used by You however You desire to use me. I yearn to accomplish the assignment You have for me in this season of singleness in my life. Father, You said that You would not leave us alone. I believe Your word. I trust Your word. Lord, when I get lonely I pray that You would comfort my heart and surround me with godly friends who will encourage me to remain obedient to You. I pray that while I am single, may You be the One to whom I am married. I pray for Your protection and that You would guard my heart against anything or anyone that would draw my attention away from You. Help me not to yield to temptation in the area of fornication, adultery, or other sexual sins. Help me to remain celibate during this season. If I am tempted, show me Your way out. It is my sincere desire not to fall into lust. I understand that my body is the temple of the Holy Spirit. I know Your Spirit will not dwell in an unclean temple. Help me to keep my temple clean. I understand that I have been bought at a price and am no longer my own. I thank You for purchasing me with Your own blood, and because of that I will honor my body. Help me to make wise decisions that would avoid alluring situations. Put other women in my life who can be confidants to me, women who will hold me accountable in my walk with You. Let me be willing to humble myself to covering from those who seek to cover me and hold me accountable in this area. Your Word declares that the joy of the Lord is my strength. Help me to be joyous as I trust You and the plan that You have for my life.

Dear Father, if at any time in my life You desire to bless me with a husband, please give me the wisdom to discern Your selection for me. Help me not to be superficial in my prayers concerning this. I realize that You know the heart of a man and You can see the part that I cannot see. Help me to trust Your decision above all. I am Yours. I am not my own, and I submit my will to You. Whatever Your plan is for me, I accept it with gladness. In Jesus' name. Amen.

Wife

The word *wife* by definition is the female partner in a marriage, but ask any husband and he will tell you that he sees the role of his wife as so much more. Genesis 2:24 says, "That is why a man leaves his father and mother and is united to his wife, and they become one flesh." In marriage, a man is instructed to leave his family and join his wife and unite with her. This means that a new home is established separate from his parents' home. This does not mean that all ties are severed with the extended family. The word *joined* speaks of both a physical embrace and more general aspects of marital bonding. In marriage, man and woman are a "we" not just a "me and you." *One flesh* suggests both a physical, sexual bonding and a lifelong relationship. They are still two persons, but together they are one.

The KJV uses the word *cleave* instead of *united*. The word *cleave* comes from the Hebrew word *dabaq*, which means to impinge, cling or adhere, to catch by pursuit, abide, fast, follow close, overtake, pursue hard, stick, or take (Strong's Concordance H1692). A closer review of the above words will help us to understand what is taking place. "A man shall leave his father and mother and [cling, adhere, abide, pursue hard] his wife." Can you imagine if the husband, after he has caught the wife by pursuit, would cling to her, forsaking all others, how joyful marriage would be. Again we have to go back to Proverbs 18:22: "Whoso findeth a wife findeth a good thing, and obtaineth favor of the Lord" (KJV). The husband is to pursue the wife. He must chase after her. God's Word never said that women are to chase after men. He is to hang on to her, accept her, and leave his father and mother. The word *leave* from the original Hebrew language *'azab* means to depart from, to abandon, forsake, neglect, to desert. (Strong Concordance H5800). While this may sound harsh, the martial relationship takes precedence over any other relationship including the child-parent relationship.

Many of the problems that exist in marriages are caused by outside interference. Some want to cleave without leaving while others want to leave without cleaving. The Scriptures are very clear on God's order for a man and his wife. This order also should be observed when children enter into the marriage. The relationship between the man and his wife takes precedence over the father with the children, as well as the mother with the children.

In Ephesians 5:31 Paul quotes from Genesis 2:24, which teaches that the special union between husband and wife supersedes the original family ties. Ephesians 5:31 is referred to as the foundation of the biblical view of marriage.

So what if God has called you to be the female partner in a marriage to one of his precious male children? What is your role? Where is the manual? Where are the instructions that will show you the way? I will use this chapter to give you valuable instructions that, if followed, will help you to become the wife that God has called you to be. When you become a wife, your mother's opinion is no longer your first line of defense.

If a woman is to be the wife that God has called her to be, then she must have a relationship with the Lord Jesus Christ. This relationship must supersede everything else in her life. Her relationship with God must be more important to her than any other relationship past, present, or future.

A wife who has a personal relationship with God will pray for her husband, and I do not mean praying asking God to change him. I mean pray with sincerity that God would have full range in his life and that the will of God would be done in his life. I must tell you that this kind of prayer may be hard to pray, and the results may be harder to accept. Because as God begins to work on the development of your husband, he may be the man of God you were not expecting. But this is the man you should seek; as a godly woman you desire a strong man of God as a mate. Many times wives will pray for their husband, and when the husband falls in love with God the wife is not prepared for the change.

Praying for your husband is necessary, especially when you do not feel like it. If you are angry with him, you need to pray for him. When he is saying things you do not like, and you want to tell him to shut up, pray for him. When you need him to finish the chore he started two years ago, pray for him. Nagging does not work! If you want the job completed, instead of nagging him, go pray for him. Prayer really does change the hearts of people, and in the process, things change as well. I cannot tell you the number of times I have had my desires met through prayer. The great thing about praying is that when God changes the husband's mind, the wife will not be able to receive the praise, but all the glory goes to God.

God can deal with your husband in a subtle way that will bring about the desired results. When a wife beats her husband down until he gives in, this is not beneficial to any of the parties involved. The wife may get what she desires, but the relationship has been bruised. Men desire respect from their wives, just as women need love. If a man does not feel respected by his wife, he feels that she does not love him.

It is very disappointing to go into a marriage thinking you can change your husband. Even if he wants to bring adjustments into his life, he may not be able to. If he is able to adjust his life, he may not be able to do it when you want him to. And if he is able to change, it may only be a temporary adjustment. People cannot change themselves. Only God can change the heart of another.

Pray for the protection of your husband; pray that God would guide and direct him. Remember, as God leads and guides your husband, the husband will lead and guide his family.

If a wife is committed to praying for her husband, she will be the greatest recipient of her own prayers. Life is always better in the household when God is the leader. When a husband has a right relationship with God, he will love his wife as Christ has instructed him in the Word of God.

If your husband is a non-believer, as a godly wife you still have a responsibility to pray for him. You have a responsibility most definitely to pray for his salvation, first and foremost, without ceasing. First Corinthians 7:13-14: "And if a woman has a husband who is not a believer and he is willing to live with her, she must not divorce him. For the unbelieving husband has been sanctified through his wife." Paul is addressing a problem here in this Scripture. Sometimes a couple will marry both as nonbelievers and the wife will receive Christ as Savior and the husband will not. Paul is giving instructions on how to handle such a situation. He writes that if the unbelieving spouse wants to stay in the marriage, then the believing spouse should not divorce him. When the unbeliever is exposed to the teaching of the Word of God, prayer, and personal witness from the spouse's lifestyle, the unbelieving mate can be won to the Lord.

The godly wife will pray for her husband in any area that she sees he is lacking in. Maybe he is not happy with his job, pray. Perhaps he is experiencing challenges in his health, pray. You can pray for any areas of his life as well and for your relationship with him. Never underestimate the power of prayer.

A godly wife is called to be an encourager to her husband. A wife should never put her husband down. Proverbs 31:11 reads "the heart of her husband safely trusts her." The word *trust* comes from the Hebrew word *batach*, which means to have confidence, to be bold, to be secure, and to feel safe (Strong's Concordance H982). Your husband needs to know he's safe around you and you will not make a negative judgment against him. He needs to be able to let his guard down, to relax and unwind and know that you will not hold any failures he might share against him. He needs to know that no matter how bad he messes up, you are still his number-one encourager. Remember you are not the Holy Spirit in his life. It is not your place to convict and sentence. If your husband is a man of God, know that God will deal with him. If he is not a believer, still know that God will also deal with him.

Your husband has to feel secure enough to confide in you. As your husband, he needs to know you will always be on his side. He needs to be able to be at ease, let his hair down, and have time to exhale. If he needs to cry, you should be his safe place to cry. He needs to be able to let you see who he really is and have confidence that you will still love him. Now I know this can be challenging because most men have not had good role models. They have not learned how to trust another person. They grew up in environments where they were told do not trust anyone. Many men feel they have to always be on guard, even with the ones they love. Many of them have darkness in their past, and they have decided within themselves that "no one will love me if they know the real me." The godly wife, through prayer, can offer a safe place for her husband to share his secrets. When your husband finally feels comfortable enough to open up to you, please, please do not utter criticisms or judgments. If you do, rest assured he probably will never open up to you again. Men have a way of disconnecting from you while still living with you. A husband can disconnect from his wife while still having sexual intercourse with her. He still caresses you, still whispers sweet nothings in your ear, but he has disconnected because of constant disapproval and continual badgering from his wife.

Can your husband trust you? Once trust has left a marriage, it is very difficult to recapture it. Even losing trust in the small things can drive a wedge between two people. Broken confidence is not easily restored.

A wife owes it to her husband to be honest with him. A relationship built on lies will not last. Many would say, if he messes up, I need to be honest with him and let him know. May I recommend you go in prayer and allow God to deal with his heart? The honesty that I speak of here has more to do with deceit. Do not lie to your husband. This does not mean that you need to point out every fault or failure he has. A man's spirit can be broken, and once it is broken it is difficult to rebuild.

Pretense and cheating will cause great problems in a marriage. Cheating is not always about an extramarital affair. When we allow our heart to be given to another, we are cheating on our husbands. In some cases it does not have to be another person. It could be a hobby or an interest that we put before our husbands.

For many who have had extramarital affairs, they will tell you it did not start out in the bedroom. There was an emotional connection first, and that is when the affair first started. I believe it is vital that we address this in the age we now live. We live in the cyber age, where many connections are made via social networking sites. Many people will never meet, but there is an emotional connection formed. When you find yourself chatting online with the opposite sex about something that you should be talking to your spouse about, you have stepped over the line.

If the husband does not trust his wife, he will be constantly questioning everything she does or says. If he cannot trust you, his wife, whom can he trust? Being honest and direct regarding feelings is very important. Share what is important to you, what you feel, what hurts you, and what pleases you. As a godly wife, do not make your husband guess or try to figure out what is bothering you. Learn to communicate effectively and make your marriage a priority.

A godly wife must have a forgiving heart. Just as in life, marriage will have its share of challenges. Situations will arise that will require forgiveness on both the part of the wife as well as the husband. Forgiveness will prevent minor frustrations from developing into major issues. Forgiveness is one of the most important things God asks of us. Forgiveness is mentioned in the Lord's Prayer: "And forgive us our debts, as we forgive our debtors." Scripture teaches on forgiveness over and over. In fact Matthew 6:15 says, "But if you do not forgive others their sins, your Father will not forgive your sins." With forgiveness, your life will be simple and full of peacefulness.

It is important that a wife respect her husband. As I stated earlier, men often equate respect to love. If you do not respect him, then he feels that you do not love him. Respect is an emotion or attitude of admiration and esteem toward someone. That does sound like love to me. Ephesians 5:33: "However, each one of you also must love his wife as he loves himself, and the wife must respect her husband." The King James Version uses the word *reverence*, which in the Greek is the word *phobeō*, which means to reverence, venerate, to treat with deference or reverential obedience. (Strong's Concordance G5399)

First Peter 3:6: "Like Sarah, who obeyed Abraham and called him her lord, you are her daughters if you do what is right and do not give way to fear" (NIV). "Even as Sara obeyed Abraham, calling him lord: whose daughters ye are, as long as ye do well, and are not afraid with any amazement" (KJV). The same Greek word *phobeō* is used for —*afraid* meaning to reverence, venerate, to treat with deference or reverential obedience. Sarah was not worshiping Abraham. She was showing him respect by calling him her lord. Fear of her husband should not be the motivating factor that causes a godly wife to respect her husband.

Paul admonishes us in Ephesians 5:22-33 regarding love and respect for each other in a marriage.

Wives, submit yourselves to your own husbands as you do to the Lord. For the husband is the head of the wife as Christ is the head of the church, his body, of which he is the Savior. Now as the church submits to Christ, so also wives should submit to their husbands in everything. Husbands, love your wives, just as Christ loved the church and gave himself up for her to make her holy, cleansing her by the washing with water through the word, and to present her to himself as a radiant church, without stain or wrinkle or any other blemish, but holy and blameless. In this same way, husbands ought to love their wives as their own bodies. He who loves his wife loves himself. After all, no one ever hated their own body, but they feed and care for their body, just as Christ does the church— for we are members of his body. "For this reason a man will leave his father and mother and be united to his wife, and the two will become one flesh." This is a profound mystery—but I am talking about Christ and the church. However, each one of you also must love his wife as he loves himself, and the wife must respect her husband.

The husband and the wife have different roles in the marriage, and the wife voluntarily submits out of her own submission to the Lord. The husband is called upon to love his wife as Christ loves the church. The husband is to have the kind of love for his wife that he is willing to lay down his life for her. He must also be willing to serve her even if it means suffering. Wives are instructed to respect their husbands. The husband will view true respect as love. Husbands need respect and wives need love; therefore, not being respectful is harmful to your relationship.

The most valuable advice I can give to a young wife is to let go of your expectations. I am not saying that you should not have expectations, but what I am saying is that many times we set ourselves up with unrealistic expectations. People will not respond to our expectations. Many men are incapable of living up to the expectations their wives have set for them. Marriage is a real life experience; we cannot look at the glamour seen on television. Not every man looks like a model, and no matter what he does he will never look like one.

We cannot look at neighbors, other believers, or even our parents as a prototype. Sure we can learn some valuable lessons from other believers, but each marriage is unique. The Word of God must be our instruction manual if we are to have marriages that honor God.

Many husbands come from broken homes with no good role models. They have little knowledge of what it means to be a good husband, and they, like many wives, are just trying to be the best they can. Some could say that women have an advantage over men in that women have played house for a number of years. In our fantasy world, we have imagined what we want our homes to be like. Little girls daydream about getting married and having children. Girls have already picked out the kind of wedding gown they want long before they will need one. There appears to be an inherited nature regarding being a wife. Men on the other hand have not given much thought to setting up a home. Their childhood thoughts were more about playing sports. So when a man gets married and he does not live up to the wife's expectations, he is somewhat in the dark as to what she was expecting. These things need to be discussed before the proposal. Each person should be willing to lay out their expectation. The unrealistic expectations will need to be adjusted before the marriage takes place. If you are already in an unfulfilled marriage and your husband is not living up to your expectation, I suggest seeking godly counsel and going into prayer. Some fasting may be necessary as well.

I grew up in a family with a dad who worked on our cars. We never went to a mechanic to have oil changes done. Dad did the oil changes in the backyard. My brothers grew up doing the same kinds of things with their cars. Every Saturday our backyard was like a car wash, with someone washing, waxing or polishing the cars. All the boys in my neighborhood who had cars had clean cars because they did the same thing my brothers did on Saturday morning. So imagine my surprise when I got married and my husband did not wash the cars. It did not take me long to figure out that if I wanted the cars washed I needed to do it myself or find out where the cheapest car wash was in town.

I quickly learned there was nothing wrong with my husband; it had to do with my expectations. Nowhere in the marriage vow did it say "thou shall wash the cars." Expectations can be our worst enemy. My husband worked hard all week, and the last thing he wanted to do on Saturday was wash a car, and I do not blame him. Now that is a very simple example, but expectations can destroy a marriage when they get out of control. What if I had complained weekly about his failure to wash the car? Pretty soon he would have gotten fed up with my moans and either washed the car or tuned me out. And if he had become the car washer of our family, is that the way I would have wanted to motivate him, through my continual protesting? I think not. It was better for me to adjust my expectations and move on.

A wife needs to learn her husband's language. Not just his love language but his language period. What does he mean when he says "I don't know?" Does that mean I do not want to talk about it, or I really do not know? It is important that you know your husband's language; otherwise you will drive yourself insane. Some husbands will expect their wives to be mind readers, but that is one of the few talents wives do not possess. Only God knows the unspoken thoughts of man.

But learning your husband's language will help to improve communication. So when you make dinner and he only eats a small portion, does that mean he does not like what you cooked, or does that mean his mind is troubled and his appetite is gone? No two men are alike. I was married for four months before I knew my husband did not like macaroni and cheese. I love macaroni and cheese, and it was one of the few things I could make with confidence, so I made it a lot, and he ate it every time. One day I was talking to his mother on the phone, and she asked me what I made for dinner and I said macaroni and cheese and she replied "none of my boys like macaroni and cheese." So when I questioned my husband later, he admitted that he did not really like it, but he knew I did and since I made it, he ate it. Now that is love. I do not believe I would have kept silent for so long if the roles had been reversed.

I probably would never be able to tell what my husband likes to eat by watching how he eats the meals I prepare. So I had to learn his language; when it came to foods that I cooked, I would have to ask before I made it, or better yet before I purchased it, if he likes it or not. The drawback of having such a pliable husband is that now, after over twenty years of marriage, if someone asks me "does your husband like...?" I sometimes do not know the answer if it is not something that I have asked him directly.

So what are the rewards of being a godly wife? The Bible gives an example in Proverbs 31:10-31. The word *virtuous* as used in the King James Version speaks of excellence, moral worth, ability, and nobility. The godly wife is blessed by her family. Her husband boasts on her. Can your husband boast about you as his wife? Have you assisted him in his growth and development of being the man that God has called him to be through prayer and encouragement? A wife plays a vital role in the successes or failures of her husband.

> A wife of noble character who can find? She is worth far more than rubies. Her husband has full confidence in her and lacks nothing of value. She brings him good, not harm, all the days of her life. She selects wool and flax and works with eager hands. She is like the merchant ships, bringing her food from afar. She gets up while it is still night; she provides

food for her family and portions for her female servants. She considers a field and buys it; out of her earnings she plants a vineyard. She sets about her work vigorously; her arms are strong for her tasks. She sees that her trading is profitable, and her lamp does not go out at night. In her hand she holds the distaff and grasps the spindle with her fingers. She opens her arms to the poor and extends her hands to the needy. When it snows, she has no fear for her household; for all of them are clothed in scarlet. She makes coverings for her bed; she is clothed in fine linen and purple. Her husband is respected at the city gate, where he takes his seat among the elders of the land. She makes linen garments and sells them, and supplies the merchants with sashes. She is clothed with strength and dignity; she can laugh at the days to come. She speaks with wisdom, and faithful instruction is on her tongue. She watches over the affairs of her household and does not eat the bread of idleness. Her children arise and call her blessed; her husband also, and he praises her: "Many women do noble things, but you surpass them all." Charm is deceptive, and beauty is fleeting; but a woman who fears the LORD is to be praised. Honor her for all that her hands have done, and let her works bring her praise at the city gate.

Proverbs 31:10-31

Prayer of a Godly Wife

Dear Heavenly Father

Help me to be the wife that You have called me
to be. Help me to honor my husband. In the
areas where I fall short, teach me how to come
up. Help me not to respond to him based on
the way he treats me. My desire is to be the wife
You have called me to be. I pray in the name
of Jesus that I would use the Word of God as
my manual. I know marriage is ordained by
You, and I believe marriage is very precious to
You. Teach me, dear Father, how to be a help
to my husband and not a hindrance. Teach me
how to love him even when I do not feel like
loving him. I know that marriage is an area of
my life where I have the opportunity to honor
You. Do not let me miss out on the awesome
privilege that has been afforded me to show
forth the love of Christ even in my marriage.
Bring us together in oneness as Your Word said
we should be. Teach us how to communicate
with one another. Help us to understand what
it means to love unconditionally. Do not let me
be the kind of wife that reiterates hurts and
disappointments over and over, but give me a
heart to forgive and to forget. Give me wisdom
to know how to love my husband during the
difficult times. Help me to always seek You for
direction when I do not understand. Help me
to pray even when I do not know what to say.
Teach me how to answer with a kind word. It
is my desire to be slow to speak. I realize that

many situations will come up in our marriage that I will want to correct immediately, but help me to wait patiently on You and to trust You in every area of our marriage. I desire to be the best wife I can to my husband. Help me to willing receive godly counsel from others. In Jesus' name I pray. Amen.

Mothers are not only the first but the greatest teachers their children will ever have. A key question to explore is: what are mothers teaching their children? In 2 Timothy 3:15 Paul writes to Timothy, "and how from infancy you have known the Holy Scriptures, which are able to make you wise for salvation through faith in Christ Jesus." Paul emphasizes Timothy's godly heritage. Timothy's mother, Eunice, and his grandmother, Lois, had faithfully taught him the Word of God. As a result of learning the truth of God's Word, Timothy had a relationship with Christ.

Mothers, of all the things we can teach our children, it means little if we fail to teach them the Word of God. We can teach them to ride a bike or drive a car, but if we fail to share the love that God has for them, we have failed our children. That might sound harsh, but it is the truth. Mothers are to love their children. How can you truly love your children and not let them know that Christ loved them so much that He died for their sins? Our children need to know that God desires a relationship with them.

In order for mothers to teach their children the Word of God, mothers must study the Word. Mothers need to be able to discuss with their children what God's plan is concerning their life. In order for a mother to be able to share with her child the plan of God, the mother needs to know God's plan for her own life. In order to assist her child in developing a walk with God, the mother has to have a relationship with God. Mothers, you cannot teach what you have no understanding of.

As you intercede for your children, ask God to reveal His plan for your life as well. A mother who is walking in the plan of God for her life will have no problem sharing God with her children.

Children learn so many things from their surroundings. It is important that the child sees the mother praying and spending time in the Word of God. The child needs to see the mother walking in purpose with a commitment to obey God.

The mother needs to have a working knowledge of the Word of God. Having a working knowledge of God's Word requires daily studying. Design a schedule that puts God's Word at the center of family activities. When you are alone with your children, devote some time to teaching them the Word of God.

Proverbs 1:8: "Listen, my son, to your father's instruction and do not forsake your mother's teaching." A theme throughout the book of Proverbs is an appeal to parents to teach their children. Both father and mother are admonished to teach their children at all times. Use every opportunity to pour into the lives of those who God has assigned to your care. Mothers, you have been given an assignment by God to teach your children.

In these last days our children are faced with many ungodly challenges. Things that were unheard of a few years ago are now constantly facing our children. Topics that were debated in high school are now being discussed in elementary school. Parents have to put their young children on guard because sin is running rampant in our world, and satan wants our offspring.

Proverbs 31:1: "The sayings of King Lemuel—an inspired utterance his mother taught him." Lemuel's mother advised him not to give his strength to women. The wisdom of his mother was that such conduct destroys leaders. She also instructed him to avoid alcoholic drink so that he could have a clear head to rule honestly.

> These commandments that I give you today are to be on your hearts. Impress them on your children. Talk about them when you sit at home and when you walk along the road, when you lie down and when you get up. Tie them as symbols on your hands and bind them on your foreheads. Write them on the doorframes of your houses and on your gates.
>
> Deuteronomy 6:6-9

God's Word should be so essential to a godly mother that she never misses an opportunity to tell of His goodness. Even while she is performing other activities she will share her love of God's Word with her children. It is a wise mother who realizes that investing time in her children will someday bring a handsome reward.

Children are a great investment for a parent. If you invest time in your children, teaching them about the things of God, it will be beneficial in the end. If the Word is planted in their hearts, they will have something to draw from when the enemy tries to speak into their life.

While riding in the car, teach the Word of God to your children. Incorporate God's Word into your playtime when the children are young. Use every moment as a teaching moment to share with them what God has to say. Bedtime prayer and nighttime reading are good, but bedtime is not the only time to share the Word with your children.

Isaiah 55:11: "So is my word that goes out from my mouth: It will not return to me empty, but will accomplish what I desire and achieve the purpose for which I sent it." When mothers use God's Word to teach their children, they can be confident that The Word of God will accomplish its purpose. For some children it may take many years to see a harvest. But the words that mother spoke in their ear will be evident by the eventual penetration of their heart. I have known many souls to come into the kingdom as a result of a mother's teaching. In some cases the mother had gone to be with the Lord, but her words still ring in the ears of her children. What an awesome privilege mothers have been given to impart God's Word into the hearts of their children.

As a mother, impartation is a huge part of what God has called us to do. Let the things that we impart to our children be God ordained. Even without trying, mothers are imparting values to their children, for they are watching everything you do. We have the opportunity to be godly examples for our children.

Mothers, teach your children how to recognize the call of God for their own lives. They are never too young to be used by God. First Samuel 2:18-21: "But Samuel was ministering before the Lord—a boy wearing a linen ephod. Each year his mother made him a little robe and took it to him when she went up with her husband to offer the annual sacrifice. Eli would bless Elkanah and his wife, saying, 'May the Lord give you children by this woman to take the place of the one she prayed for and gave to the Lord.' Then they would go home. And the Lord was gracious to Hannah; she gave birth to three sons and two daughters. Meanwhile, the boy Samuel grew up in the presence of the Lord."

Hannah gave her son Samuel to God just as she had vowed to do, and he began ministering before the Lord at an early age. The Word of the Lord was rare in those days. The Scriptures show us how God used the boy Samuel as well as the Prophet Samuel.

What are mothers today teaching their children? Are mothers instilling a love for the things of the world or a love for the things of God? Mothers have it within their scope of influence to produce godly children or ungodly children. This is not to say that all children will develop as we want them to, but we must take responsibility for our roles in the lives of our children. Mothers are their children's first and most persuasive teachers. This is a responsibility that must be taken very seriously.

Training of a child plays a crucial role in children developing and maturing into adults who can contribute to the cause of Christ. It is not the responsibility of the daycare or teacher to train our children. It is not the responsibility of the youth pastor either. Although we appreciate others coming beside to assist in child rearing, it is still the primary responsibility of the parents, a charge that mothers cannot take frivolously.

Mothers, make a commitment to be present in the lives of your children. They cannot raise themselves. Show up for your children; they need you to have a daily presence in their lives. Mothers, monitor your child's television viewing time. Limit their video game playing and computer time. Encourage them to read good books. Spend time talking with them about things that are on their mind. Help them to navigate through the maze of life. God will hold us accountable for how we raise our children. When mothers stand before God and He asks "what did you do with the children I gave you?" what will our response be? We will not be able to blame society as Adam and Eve cast blame in the garden when God questioned Adam. Eve blamed the serpent, and Adam blamed Eve. As mothers we have to be mature enough to deny ourselves some luxuries in order to develop the character of our children.

You may want to go to bed early and sleep late, but as a mother we have to be on duty to assist our children. They do not have the skill set to make decisions that need to be made. Talk with your children, and let them know they can come to you with questions. It is so important to establish the proper relationship with children at an early age. They need to know that you will always be their mother first. Most children really do depend on their parents for guidance.

Mothers, it is so important that we begin to speak words of affirmation over our children when they are very young. This life-defining declaration for a little girl can be life altering. We have to affirm over and over that they are God's special design and that He has a plan for their lives.

Words have great power, especially when they are used by someone in authority. The Bible teaches about the tongue and how damaging it can be. Proverbs 18:21: "The tongue has the power of life and death, and those who love it will eat its fruit." Mothers can speak life to their children or they can speak death to them.

James 3:5-6: "Likewise, the tongue is a small part of the body, but it makes great boasts. Consider what a great forest is set on fire by a small spark. The tongue also is a fire, a world of evil among the parts of the body. It corrupts the whole body, sets the whole course of one's life on fire, and is itself set on fire by hell." James is teaching the hearers the devastating results of an uncontrolled tongue. He says the tongue defiles the whole body. The whole course of a child's life can be damaged by an untamed mother's tongue.

Learn to speak blessings over your child's life. The child may be disobedient, but bring correction in love. Reaffirm to the child how valuable they are to you and to God. Let them know how much they are loved, but remember to bring necessary correction as well. Do not allow your children to desecrate their bodies. Show them how to take care of themselves both physically and emotionally. Teach them how to dress appropriately for their age. Many times mothers assume their children know things. But they do not know as much as we think they know. After all where would they learn it, from television? We must teach our children our values. The world's values are different from the values of a believer; let's not leave it up to the world to instill values in our children. They are a precious gift from God on loan to us for the purpose of preparing them to return back to the Father when He calls.

Perhaps you are unable to have biological children, and you feel the urging of the Lord that motherhood is for you. Consider adoption; there are many children who would benefit from the instructions of a lovely, adoptive mother. Be willing to share the love and the joy that God has placed in your heart. Foster care is another option that will allow a woman to experience motherhood. There also may be children in your extended family or your church family whose lives you could make a difference in. Do not feel that because you have not given birth physically that you cannot be a mother. There are millions of children whose lives can be touched by women who did not give birth to them. The lives of these children will be forever changed by godly women willing to invest in them in some way or another.

It is an awesome experience to be able to deposit something meaningful into the life of a child. Children are precious, and when a mother takes the time to teach and train them according to the Word of God, the returns will be evident. It takes time to train children. It cannot be left up to them to decide what they should or should not do.

Children do not have the reasoning ability to make important decisions for their own lives. There is nothing wrong with letting a child make insignificant decisions, but the final decision should always be left to the parent.

Think back to when you were a child and some of the decisions you made. Would you make the same decision now as an adult? Most likely not. Some researchers have stated that the brain does not fully develop until the age of twenty-five. Think about decisions you made before the age of twenty-five and if you would make the same decision today at forty-five.

As mothers, we have to be willing to step into the gap and make the necessary decisions for our children. This is not to say the child cannot be involved in the decision-making process, but ultimately the parent is responsible. God did not call you to be your child's best friend, but to be their instructor. Teaching and training must be forever in the thoughts of parents looking at each situation to see how it can be used as a teaching opportunity. Teachable moments come in many forms; do not allow one to go overlooked by you.

Mothers need to be good listeners. Take an interest in what is on your child's mind. Learn to listen when your child is speaking. Offer suggestions and comments when appropriate, but listen more than you talk. Sometimes listening is the only thing that is needed.

If you are blessed with more than one child, remember each child is different. One may talk too much, and the other may not talk much at all. Learn the temperament of your children. Avoid comparing them to each other; each one is God's original design. He has a unique purpose for each child. Your children may have totally different personalities, but embrace their interests. Help them to discover what they are good at. They will not be good in everything, and it is important that they learn how to fail but not give up.

When disciplining is needed, it may be different for each child. One child may respond to a stern voice while the other may require a more forceful form of discipline. Something may need to be taken away from one child in order to teach him about sharing while the other child may only require an explanation. Be flexible; know your child. You will learn your child by spending time talking and listening to what is on his or her heart.

Training needs to start early in the life of a child. Do not wait until a child is two years old to start teaching them. Lessons can be taught at each stage of development. Remember to use appropriate techniques for each age group. Removing a two-year-old from a high stimulant environment may calm him down. But when a child is sixteen, you cannot always remove him from stimulating environments. In many cases he will need to know how to adjust. Help your child to determine what coping mechanism he can use to calm himself when in a stressful situation.

Jesus said in Matthew 19:13, "Then people brought little children to Jesus for him to place his hands on them and pray for them. But the disciples rebuked them. Jesus said, 'Let the little children come to me, and do not hinder them, for the kingdom of heaven belongs to such as these.' When he had placed his hands on them, he went on from there. Jesus blessed the little children." They were important to Him.

Mothers, if children are that important to Jesus, it tells us a little about the trust He has placed in you to take care of His little children. Being a mother is a high calling from God. He entrusted a precious possession to mothers, little children. To be used by God to bring a child into the world is phenomenal. But even more significant is how we nurture and cultivate the child that we have been gifted with.

Hannah was barren, and God opened her womb and gave her Samuel. Hannah was faithful to keep her vow to God. She understood the gift she had been given and gave the gift back to God. Her husband, Elkanah, loved her, and the Scripture teaches that, "But to Hannah he gave a double portion because he loved her, and the Lord had closed her womb." First Samuel 1:5

Hannah prayed unto the Lord, and she vowed a vow to God. Hannah vowed that if God would give her a male child that she would give him back to the Lord all the days of his life. Mothers, it is important that we understand that our children come from God and that we have to be willing to dedicate them back to God.

"After he was weaned, she took the boy with her, young as he was, along with a three-year-old bull, an ephah of flour and a skin of wine, and brought him to the house of the Lord at Shiloh. When the bull had been sacrificed, they brought the boy to Eli, and she said to him, "Pardon me, my lord. As surely as you live, I am the woman who stood here beside you praying to the Lord. I prayed for this child, and the Lord has granted me what I asked of him. So now I give him to the Lord. For his whole life he will be given over to the Lord." And he worshiped the Lord there. When Hannah had weaned the child, she took him up with her to the house of the Lord in Shiloh. She brought the child to Eli and said, "for this child I prayed; and the Lord heard me." First Samuel 1:24-28. Hannah offers Samuel back to the Lord and as Samuel is ministering unto the Lord, he hears the voice of God.

> The boy Samuel ministered before the Lord under Eli. In those days the word of the Lord was rare; there were not many visions. One night Eli, whose eyes were becoming so weak that he could barely see, was lying down in his usual place. The lamp of God had not yet gone out, and Samuel was lying down in the house of the Lord, where the ark of God was. Then the Lord called Samuel. Samuel answered, "Here I am." And he ran to Eli and said, "Here I am; you called me." But Eli said, "I did not call; go back and lie down." So he went and lay down. Again the Lord called, "Samuel!" And Samuel

got up and went to Eli and said, "Here I am; you called me." "My son," Eli said, "I did not call; go back and lie down." Now Samuel did not yet know the Lord: The word of the Lord had not yet been revealed to him. A third time the Lord called, "Samuel!" And Samuel got up and went to Eli and said, "Here I am; you called me." Then Eli realized that the Lord was calling the boy. So Eli told Samuel, "Go and lie down, and if he calls you, say, 'Speak, Lord, for your servant is listening.'"

1 Samuel 3:1-10

God called Samuel when there was not much prophetic movement, perhaps because there were so few faithful Israelites who would listen. Three times Samuel ran to the priest because he did not recognize it was God calling him. Samuel was young, and he did not yet know the voice of God. He had never received God's Word by divine revelation.

Eli realized what was happening. Eli knew God was speaking to Samuel. Mothers, your children may not know when God is calling them, but a godly mother will be able to instruct her children concerning the call of God regarding their life.

Eli told Samuel, the next time you hear the voice say "speak Lord, your servant is listening." First Samuel 3:9. Just as God called young Samuel, He is calling young people today.

Mothers, teach your children and prepare them for the work of ministry so that when God calls they will be ready to answer. When you talk with them, ask them if they have heard God calling them? Many of the adults I know who are now involved in ministry say they knew from the time of childhood that God was calling them. I often wonder if someone, perhaps a mother, would have taken the time to talk and explore the call of God with them, if that individual could have been further along in ministry.

Children are a gift from God. When God gives a gift, it is a blessing, but it is also a responsibility. The role of a mother is key in the life of a child. Mothers are there when the child is sick. Mothers are there when the child goes off to college and to help the bride plan her wedding. Mothers are there for the grandchildren. The role of the mother is never finished. When a mother blesses her children and directs them to a relationship with Jesus Christ, she has fulfilled her most important call. God will bless mothers and reward them for being good stewards over the gifts He has given them, their children.

Some children unfortunately grow up without the tender touch of a loving mother. They are born into families with abuse, low self-esteem, self-haters, etc. A child who has not had the attention of a loving mother will miss many essential lessons in life. But that is one of the reasons, I believe, that God has placed mothers in the body of Christ, not only to teach the younger women, but to teach women who have not had the intimate relationship of an earthly mother who could instruct them on how to be mothers to their own children.

Mothers, let us take our responsibility seriously, whether it is our own children or others that God has placed in our life. Teach them what God requires of them as young women and as young mothers. The curse of abuse, low self-esteem, and self-haters can stop with you. If you are a mother and you are reading this chapter, please be motivated to extend your arms of love to someone you know that may not have a godly mother. I have included some Scriptures to remind you just how valuable you are to the children of the kingdom.

> Honor your father and your mother, as the LORD your God has commanded you, so that you may live long and that it may go well with you in the land the LORD your God is giving you.
>
> Deuteronomy 5:16

> He settles the childless woman in her home as a happy mother of children.
>
> Psalm 113:9

> Children are a heritage from the LORD, offspring a reward from him. Like arrows in the hands of a warrior are children born in one's youth. Blessed is the man whose quiver is full of them. They will not be put to shame when they contend with their opponents in court.
>
> Psalm 127:3-5

> Hear, my son, your father's instruction, and forsake not your mother's teaching, for they are a graceful garland for your head and pendants for your neck.

Proverbs 1:8-9

My son, keep your father's commandment, and forsake not your mother's teaching. Bind them on your heart always; tie them around your neck. When you walk, they will lead you; when you lie down, they will watch over you; and when you awake, they will talk with you.

Proverbs 6:20-22

A wise son brings joy to his father, but a foolish son brings grief to his mother.

Proverbs 10:1

A good person leaves an inheritance for their children's children, but a sinner's wealth is stored up for the righteous.

Proverbs 13:22

Children's children are a crown to the aged, and parents are the pride of their children.

Proverbs 17:6

The righteous lead blameless lives; blessed are their children after them.

Proverbs 20:7

If someone curses their father or mother, their lamp will be snuffed out in pitch darkness.

Proverbs 20:20

Listen to your father, who gave you life, and do not despise your mother when she is old. Buy the truth and do not sell it— wisdom, instruction and insight as well. The father of a righteous child has great joy; a man who fathers a wise son rejoices in him. May your father and mother rejoice; may she who gave you birth be joyful!

Proverbs 23:22-25

Her children stand and bless her. Her husband praises her.

Proverbs 31:28

As one whom his mother comforts, so I will comfort you; And you will be comforted in Jerusalem.

Isaiah 66:13

Children, obey your parents in the Lord, for this is right. Honor your father and mother—which is the first commandment with a promise— so that it may go well with you and that you may enjoy long life on the earth.

Ephesians 6:1-3

A Mother's Prayer

Dear Heavenly Father

Thank You for the precious gift You have given me, my children. I realize that they belong to You and You have entrusted me to bring them up in the ways of the Lord. What a privilege to have this opportunity to pour into Your children. I realize that whatever I invest in my children, I will not lose, but I will be rewarded.

Their minds are fresh and pure; I thank You for blessing our family with these little ones. I place these children in Your hands. I pray for wisdom to teach them Your ways. I pray for strength to be an example before them.

Help me to teach them through the Word of God what it means to be a believer so that when they come to an understanding of who You are, they will receive You as their personal Savior.

I pray that every need that they have will be met as they trust You to perform Your Word in their lives. Thank You God for assigning me the responsibility of caring for Your most treasured gift. Dear Lord, I ask that You would allow me to see other children who may not have a mother's love. Help me to stand in the gap as I pray for them. And when opportunity presents itself, help me to be ready to answer the call of motherhood that is on my life. I give myself to be used by You as a mother to the motherless in any way You see necessary. In Jesus' name I pray. Amen.

Ministry

In today's society, some are still questioning the views held by the Christian church. One of the issues still in question is the role of women in ministry. While some churches have settled this matter, others still are not quite sure. Some are not sure what to do with women who say they have been called by God to ministry. What do we do with these women? What area of ministry can they be used in?

First Corinthians 14:34-35 reads, "Women should remain silent in the churches. They are not allowed to speak, but must be in submission, as the law says. If they want to inquire about something, they should ask their own husbands at home; for it is disgraceful for a woman to speak in the church."

Paul's words here are the subject of much debate because it seems to be the opposite of what Paul spoke in 1 Corinthians 11:5: "But every woman who prays or prophesies with her head uncovered dishonors her head—it is the same as having her head shaved." Women were permitted to pray and prophesy in the assembly, otherwise Paul would have no need to give instructions regarding this matter. Paul was addressing a particular problem in the Corinthian church. First Corinthians was written by Paul to set things in order while He was in Ephesus, during his third missionary journey. Paul was responding to letters he received from the Corinthian believers. The church at Corinth was out of order in many regards. One of the subjects that Paul had to address was spiritual gifts, because the church of Corinth was operating in the gifts, but there was no order.

As one reads the Bible, there is adequate evidence in Scripture of women and how Jesus related to them. Some of these women were used by Him to relay His message to others.

In John 4, Jesus met a woman at the well, and this woman leaves her water pots at the well to run and tell others about her encounter with Jesus.

Jesus had left Judea and had gone back once more to Galilee. "Now he had to go through Samaria. So he came to a town in Samaria called Sychar, near the plot of ground Jacob had given to his son Joseph. Jacob's well was there, and Jesus, tired as he was from the journey, sat down by the well. It was about noon. When a Samaritan woman came to draw water, Jesus said to her, 'Will you give me a drink?' (His disciples had gone into the town to buy food)" John 4:4-8. As Jesus rested at Jacob's well and the others went for food, there came a woman to draw water.

The Samaritan woman did not come to the well at the customary time in the cool of the evening with the other women but came alone earlier in the day, around noon. It is not given to us in Scripture why this woman came to the well at this odd time.

Perhaps she came intentionally at this time because she knew no one else would be at the well. After all she did not have a glowing reputation among the other townspeople, as Jesus would later reveal. Her character may have made her unpopular with the other women in the town, and she wanted to avoid their pointing and staring. It is a common thing even in our society today to avoid those who do not welcome our company.

This woman, no doubt, had been ignored by the others at the usual water drawing time and had made up her mind that she could not deal with it anymore. So she made her own schedule for drawing water when she knew no one else would be at the well.

But when she arrives at the well, she is in for quite a surprise. The Samaritan woman comes to the well at the right time. Although her reasons for coming at noon had nothing to do with Jesus, her chance meeting with Jesus would make all the difference in her life. This visitor who sat at the well would prove to be the best reason ever for coming to the well at noon. This woman's encounter with the Savior would turn her life completely around. It was very unusual for a Jewish teacher to talk with women in a public place, but watch what Jesus does. He asks the Samaritan woman for a drink of water. The woman was a little taken aback by the request. She pointed out that the Jews and the Samaritans did not mingle with each other. Jesus did not leave her wondering, but He responded to the Samaritan woman's statement. Jesus answered her, "If you knew the gift of God and who it is that asks you for a drink, you would have asked him and he would have given you living water." John 4:10

The living water that Jesus spoke of was eternal life. The woman did not understand Jesus' spiritual message. Naturally, she saw a thirsty stranger sitting by the well without anything to draw water with. He did not have a pitcher or cup, so how was he going to give her water from the deep well? Jesus boldly claimed to be able to permanently satisfy the thirst of her soul. The woman not clearly comprehending, perhaps hoping, said "give me this water." If Jesus could give her water that would last forever, at least it would end her daily trips to the well carrying the heavy water pots.

Jesus mentioned the woman's husband in order to expose her life to her. When an individual meets Jesus, He brings one face to face with one's sins. Sin must be brought to the light and exposed. It must be confessed so that one can receive forgiveness. In order to overcome any failure, it must first be acknowledged.

> Jesus answered, "Everyone who drinks this water will be thirsty again, but whoever drinks the water I give them will never thirst. Indeed, the water I give them will become in them a

spring of water welling up to eternal life." The woman said to him, "Sir, give me this water so that I won't get thirsty and have to keep coming here to draw water." He told her, "Go, call your husband and come back." "I have no husband," she replied. Jesus said to her, "You are right when you say you have no husband. The fact is, you have had five husbands, and the man you now have is not your husband. What you have just said is quite true."

John 4:13-18

Because of what Jesus told her about herself, the woman concluded that Jesus must be a prophet. Prophets were men divinely inspired with supernatural knowledge. The woman goes on to mention worship sites, perhaps trying to take the focus off of her situation. Maybe she realized that she was a sinner and knew that she was required to offer a sacrifice. Jesus explained to her that God is not limited by time and place. When an individual receives Jesus by faith, that individual can pray to God anywhere. As believers we understand that worship is a matter of the heart, and it is not confined to a space or time. Worship touches the heart of God; it is an expression from our heart to His heart. Worship is a time when believers can proclaim the awesomeness of who God is and declare His goodness. True worship requires a relationship with God.

After the Samaritan woman's encounter with the Savior, she became an enthusiastic witness to others who knew her. In her excitement, the woman ran to tell of her experience. That is what happens when we have been called by God. We get excited and are anxious to share the news with everyone we meet.

Many of the Samaritans from the town believed in Jesus because of what the woman told them. Could this be the same woman with a tainted reputation? Surely if she was proclaiming Christ, they had to see for themselves what was going on.

> "Come see a man who told me everything I ever did. Could this be the Messiah?" They came out of the town and made their way toward him. Meanwhile his disciples urged him, "Rabbi, eat something." But he said to them, "I have food to eat that you know nothing about." Then his disciples said to each other, "Could someone have brought him food?" "My food," said Jesus, "is to do the will of him who sent me and to finish his work. Don't you have a saying, 'It's still four months until harvest'? I tell you, open your eyes and look at the fields! They are ripe for harvest. Even now the one who reaps draws a wage and harvests a crop for eternal life, so that the sower and the reaper may be glad together. Thus the saying 'One sows and another reaps' is true. I sent you to reap what you have not worked for. Others have done the hard work, and you have reaped the benefits of their labor." Many of the Samaritans from that town believed in him because of the woman's testimony, "He told me everything I ever did." So when the Samaritans came to him, they urged him to stay with them, and he stayed two days. And because of his words many more became believers. They said to the woman, "We no longer believe just because of what you said; now we have heard for

ourselves, and we know that this man really is the
Savior of the world."

John 4:29-42

I am sure the Samaritan woman on her way to the
well did not envision such a life-changing experience.
When God calls a woman to ministry, it is indeed a
life-changing experience. Jesus asked this woman about
her husband in an effort to expose her sin. Many times
we live in sin because we can get away with it. But once
sin has been exposed, it must be dealt with.

This woman got excited as a result of her encounter
with Jesus. In her urgency she ran to tell the news. She
did not report what Jesus actually told her but what He
could have said. Her first response to Him was "You are
a Jew." Then she moved to "I perceive you are a prophet."
And finally she said, "Could this be the Messiah?" God
can use anyone who will receive His call. The Samaritan
woman, by many people's standards, probably was not
a valid candidate for the work of ministry. But God
selected her nevertheless. God is still calling women to
the work of ministry.

It was necessary that Jesus go through Samaria if
He wanted to travel the direct route to Galilee. Jesus
left Judea to avoid the controversy over baptism. The
fact that Jesus was convincing men to become disciples
had created a jealousy among those who were following
John. So Jesus left Judea and headed to Galilee. The
shortest route from Judea in the south to Galilee in the
north was to go through Samaria. Many of the Jews
would avoid going through Samaria because of the

hatred between the Jews and the Samaritans. That is why the Samaritan woman responded the way she did when Jesus spoke to her.

The bad blood between the Samaritans and the Jews went back to the days of the exile when the northern kingdom was exiled to Assyria. The king of Assyria repopulated the area with hostages from other lands. So when the immigrants and the Jews who had remained in the land married one another, it complicated the lineage of the Samaritans. The Jews despised the Samaritans and measured them to be no longer "unpolluted" Jews. Fortunately for the woman at the well, Jesus did not feel this way about the Samaritans. He called her, and she answered the call and brought others to the Messiah.

Women were used by Jesus after His resurrection. The women at the tomb were given an important message to deliver, Jesus has risen!

> After the Sabbath, at dawn on the first day of the week, Mary Magdalene and the other Mary went to look at the tomb. There was a violent earthquake, for an angel of the Lord came down from heaven and, going to the tomb, rolled back the stone and sat on it. His appearance was like lightning, and his clothes were white as snow. The guards were so afraid of him that they shook and became like dead men. The angel said to the women, "Do not be afraid, for I know that you are looking for Jesus, who was crucified. He is not here; he has risen, just as he said. Come and see the place where he lay. Then go quickly and tell his disciples: 'He has risen from the dead and is going ahead of you into Galilee. There you will

see him.' Now I have told you." So the women
hurried away from the tomb, afraid yet filled with
joy, and ran to tell his disciples. Suddenly Jesus
met them. "Greetings," he said. They came to him,
clasped his feet and worshiped him. Then Jesus
said to them, "Do not be afraid. Go and tell my
brothers to go to Galilee; there they will see me."

Matthew 28:1-10

The women were at the tomb to anoint the body
of Jesus. The angel gave the message to the women to
deliver to the disciples. The women were to tell the
disciples "He is risen as He said." As the women went,
Jesus met them and reiterated the message they were to
deliver. They were to tell the disciples that Jesus would
meet them in Galilee. Galilee was the chosen setting
for Jesus' appointment with His disciples. Our Savior
used women to carry the message of His resurrection.

Not everyone called by God is endowed with the
ministry gifts listed in Ephesians 4:11-12: "So Christ
himself gave the apostles, the prophets, the evangelists,
the pastors and teachers, to equip his people for works
of service, so that the body of Christ may be built up"
(KJV). "And he gave some, apostles; and some, prophets;
and some, evangelists; and some, pastors and teachers;
for the perfecting of the saints, for the work of the
ministry, for the edifying of the body of Christ:"

He gave some apostles or ambassadors, some prophets who delivered direct revelations from God.
Other ministry gifts that He gave to some include
evangelists, pastors, and teachers. Gifted leaders are
responsible for the equipping of the saints. God's plan

is that His church be fully armored. Those who have been given gifts must remember that the gifts are to be used for the building of the body of Christ and not for individual gain.

What area of ministry do you believe God is calling you to function in? Many women feel called to pulpit ministry. Pulpit ministry would be ministry done from the pulpit. The most obvious example of that would be the pastor of a local assembly. All would agree that the role of the pulpit ministry in the existence of the church is unequivocally necessary to the strength and well-being of the church as a whole. Teaching for everyday living is most often done from the pulpit. Sometimes it is on a Sunday morning; other times it may be in a midweek service.

Teaching the Word of God is the most important responsibility of the church. Whether it's on Sunday morning, in Bible study, or in Sunday school class, teaching the Word of God helps people learn what is expected of them as believers.

It is also through the teaching of the Word of God that many will receive understanding and accept the Lord Jesus Christ as Savior. In the book of Acts, when people heard the message and believed, they began to fellowship with one another.

> They devoted themselves to the apostles' teaching and to fellowship, to the breaking of bread and to prayer. Everyone was filled with awe at the many wonders and signs performed by the apostles. All the believers were together and had everything in common. They sold

property and possessions to give to anyone who had need. Every day they continued to meet together in the temple courts. They broke bread in their homes and ate together with glad and sincere hearts, praising God and enjoying the favor of all the people. And the Lord added to their number daily those who were being saved.

Acts 2:42-47

Teaching is the main focus of the church. We go out to win the lost and bring them in to be taught. The true passion of the church is not what many churches focus on today, but preaching and teaching the Word of God so that the lives of those who receive can be forever changed. That is the true history of the church. Many congregations have walked away from the fundamentals of the gospel. Many focus on things that bring instant and personal gratification, but we must remain true to the calling, and that is to win sinners to Jesus.

The apostle Paul told Timothy that the church was the pillar and ground of the truth (1 Timothy 3:15). Paul wrote this first letter to Timothy to give him instruction on how the local assembly and its leaders should function. The church, established by Christ, is the substance upon which the truth of God stands, specifically the Word of God as revealed in Scripture. Most—if not all—local assemblies have a senior pastor or at least a preacher who has been appointed to be focused and to present themselves approved to God, "a worker who does not need to be ashamed, rightly dividing the word of truth" (2 Timothy 2:15). *Approved* is what remains when everything else fails. *To rightly divide* means to cut it straight. Those called to pulpit ministry must not compromise the Word of God. The preacher has to be able to stand and deliver the Word straight from the Bible with no hidden agenda. The bulk of this responsibility falls on the pastor. It is the pastor's job, in the local assembly among the people of God, to "rightly divide the word of truth." The pastor is not to be consumed with other worldly matters or commitments. The pastor must give adequate time for studying and preparing so that he can instruct the people of God from the Word of God. It is a dangerous thing to serve in pulpit ministry and not be equipped. Those who serve in pulpit ministry do the people of God damage when they have not adequately prepared themselves to deliver the Word of God.

If an individual believes God is calling them to pulpit ministry, much time and dedication must be given to prayer and preparation. The servant who functions in the role of pulpit ministry has the capacity to touch every area of the ministry. Every ministry, program, and committee of the church somehow relates back to, or can be influenced by, the pulpit ministry of the church. A strong, understandable presentation of the Word of God is necessary in the pulpit ministry. It is the minster behind the pulpit that sets the attitude and the atmosphere of everything else that takes place in the local ministry.

Pulpit ministry or teaching ministry can also take place in the Sunday school, youth ministry, and other areas where instruction regarding the Word of God is being delivered. It is vital that those called to ministry understand that the bulk of what they do as ministers will be done away from the pulpit in the church. A church only needs one senior pastor. It is not wise, as a minister called by God, to sit and wait for your opportunity to minister from the pulpit. Depending on how many ministers are on the ministerial staff, you may not have the opportunity to minister very often. The work of the minister is more than a Sunday morning message from the pulpit.

Preparation for pulpit ministry will include some theology training. If God is calling you in this area, begin preparation now. The person who has been called to an office in the church is not to merely speak on matters of theology but to see that real service takes place. Meet and talk with your current pastor for counsel and prayer. It is not about popularity but about bringing the Word of God correctly.

Be true to your authentic self. When God called you, He called *you*. You are not called to preach or teach like someone else. Many women feel they have to preach like a man, using a deep voice and male mannerisms. Women sometimes feel they must adorn themselves with male attire if they are going to preach the Gospel.

Maintain your femininity as you fulfill the call of God for your life. You can be a successful woman in ministry by being exactly who God called you to be. God called you because He wants to use you as a woman to accomplish His purpose on the earth.

Attentiveness and integrity are necessary. God is calling women to ministry but only some women to pulpit ministry. If a woman wants to be sure that she has been called to pulpit ministry, she needs to pray, read the Bible, meditate, seek counsel with godly people, and listen to the voice of God. If you step out into ministry without counsel from your spiritual leader, you are out of order.

After you have spoken to your pastor, you must continue to serve where you are until God releases you to move on. Do not go to your pastor one day to discuss your calling and leave the next. Allow your spiritual leader to mentor and pour into you what is necessary for the journey that is ahead. Even after you go out on your own in ministry, you will still need the oversight of a pastor. Covering is necessary for a ministry leader; maintain a relationship with your pastor if at all possible. Your pastor, if he or she is a true man or woman of God, and if you have been with him or her for any length of time, will know you better than anyone else when it comes to spiritual things. Your pastor will be able to pray with you when you need to make decisions. If your pastor is a deeply spiritual individual, he or she will be able to discern the call of God for your life and many times will know before you do that God has called you.

The calling to minister the Word is a serious calling, and it is something you need to be absolutely sure about. James 3:1-2: "Not many of you should become teachers, my fellow believers, because you know that we who teach will be judged more strictly. We all stumble in many ways. Anyone who is never at fault in what they say is perfect, able to keep their whole body in check." Teachers of the Word will stand before the condemnation seat of Christ and be held accountable.

This means that teachers have a higher degree of responsibility for what they speak. A teacher must be diligent in prayer and preparation to speak what thus said the Lord. It is vital that those who teach the Word of God spend quality time studying the Word. If God has called you to teach, there will always be people who will take heed to what you have to say. Be sure that you are teaching the truth of God's Word with a clear understanding that others can comprehend.

God equips those He has called to the ministry. The ultimate goal is to build up the body of Christ. Women who make themselves available can be used greatly by God; it is only because of His power and Him working through those He has chosen.

When we talk about the call of God to women for ministry, it is important to realize the different calls to ministry. Not all are called to preach the gospel from the pulpit. Pulpit ministry looks attractive to those who observe from the outside. Women must remember that before God calls us to ministry, He calls us to salvation and servanthood.

When we speak about a woman's call to ministry, we have to look at her service as well as the function of the call. Knowing your specific call to ministry will determine how you function in ministry. We will talk about servanthood later.

The call from God brings tranquility to your life and to the ministry that God has called you to. That is not to say that life will be calm, but to say that your spirit will be at peace as you walk in obedience. When an individual has been called to ministry, it is first a ministry of service. As an individual desiring to be used by God as a minister of the gospel, you should already be serving in your local ministry. There are functions within the ministry of the local body, and God desires that each one function within their calling. There are many tasks required for a ministry to operate effectively. Just showing up on Sunday is not ministry. Ministry is helping one another. Ministry is serving in areas where you see a need in your local assembly. Do not wait to be asked. If you see something needs to be done, get busy serving. If it is an area that you do not oversee, then speak to the proper person to see how you can be of service. Start by being faithful where you are. If your job is to clean the restrooms, serve faithfully. If you are a nursery worker, serve faithfully. A greeter, announcer, choir member, meal server during events, whatever you are doing, do it faithfully.

Faithfulness is a requirement to serve in ministry. One must prove themselves faithful. If a person is not faithful, how can God use that person and elevate them in ministry? Start with faithful service where you are, and allow the Holy Spirit to equip you with the gifts necessary to function in ministry.

Commitment is something that must be a priority in the life of a person called to ministry. These are characteristics that need to be visible before a person can be used in ministry. Before a woman can function in ministry, she must be faithful to her leader and have a strong commitment to the local ministry. If she is married, she needs to be a faithful wife to her husband. If she is a mother, she needs to be a faithful mother to her children. Each component of a woman's life will need to be addressed before she moves into ministry. God has to be first, family second, and professional ministry needs to be third. It is easy to get caught up in the work of ministry and not be able to discern the differences between a strong relationship with God versus serving in ministry. Just because one spends long hours functioning in ministry does not mean one's relationship with God is solid. If a person is not careful, ministry can become more of a chore than a calling, and burnout can occur.

One needs to be aware of the inner calling that is God speaking to the heart. The calling needs to be validated by the confirmation of those who know you. That is why it is necessary to counsel with your spiritual leader. God can also speak to you through the spoken word from any godly leader.

Women in ministry will face some challenges in their mission to follow the plan of God for their lives. Women who are called to ministry face the challenge of building good relationships. These relationships can be hard to form, hard to maintain, and easy to destroy. The ministry lifestyle is busy and fast-paced. Many who serve in ministry do not have time to cultivate relationships on the level needed to enrich their lives. Although one will receive purposeful fulfillment from relationships built as a result of ministry, there needs to be a time of relaxation. You will need people in your life whose company you enjoy. People who will allow you time to be at ease. Those who can nurture you as God replenishes your Spirit will also be needed.

Serving in ministry can be very time consuming. It is highly encouraged that one take time to build good foundational relationships. These will be needed along the way, and it is best to build them before you become recognized in ministry. When you are recognized in ministry, many times people will want to attach themselves to you just because of who they think you are. Those relationships can be self-serving and superficial. As one serves in ministry there will be times when the love and confidence of a good friend is needed, with no strings attached.

Another challenge women face in ministry is losing focus of their own health while caring for others. Because of the nature of the personality of those called to serve in ministry, it is important not to neglect one's own health in the process of serving. It is easy for those who serve to put others before themselves. Striking a balance will be necessary to maintain and continue to be effective in ministry. Learn to take time to relax. Just because you are in ministry does not mean you have to work all day every day. Set boundaries, as there are other duties that you will have whether it be family or other responsibilities. Learn to delegate; God has placed others in the body of Christ to help.

Ministry can consume you and overwhelm you. The ministry can take on a life of its own, and you can lose yourself in the process. When you go home, like any other job, do not take your work home with you. The work of the ministry is very rewarding, and it is easy to be obsessed with the call of God. If one is going to be able to go the distance in ministry, one must demonstrate balance.

If one starts out working all the time without balance in ministry, that individual will not last long. There has to be balance even in ministry. It is better to pace oneself so that one can last until the end.

Many women in ministry experience loneliness in their lives. Women in ministry have many responsibilities and often avoid social interaction. With no social interaction, they may begin to experience a void in their lives. When loneliness sets in, it will cause you to think wrong thoughts and many times compromise the Word of God. Some will begin to say what people want to hear just to get the crowd and to be popular with the people.

Women who serve in ministry need to have accountability partners. Married women as well as single women need someone to hold them responsible. If you are a woman in ministry who travels, much wisdom is needed. That is why it is so important that you have a mentor or a spiritual leader who can advise you. Try not to travel alone if at all possible. Take extreme care not to travel with someone of the opposite sex unless you are related to that person, or you are traveling in a group.

It is important that when you travel, you have a home base, preferably a God-centered church family who can keep you covered in prayer while you travel. Maintain a good relationship with your pastor! Your pastor will be able to advise you in areas that may be new to you. Your pastor will be a good resource for problem solving, especially if he or she has experience in itinerate ministry. No matter how God develops and promotes you in ministry, never underestimate the impact of your local pastor. Your pastor has the potential to pour much into your life as you proceed to fulfill the call of God for your life.

God is using women today in all areas of ministry. If you are a women who feels the call of God to ministry, do not be afraid to step out in what God has called you to do. Seek Him and godly counseling, and you can be successful in fulfilling the call of God for your life. God is still calling women and men to a higher level of commitment for His purpose in the gospel ministry.

A Minister's Prayer

Dear Heavenly Father,

I come now in the name of Jesus. I believe that You have called me to the gospel ministry. I pray that You would search my heart as You prepare me to walk in Your plan for my life. Please direct me to the people I should seek out as mentors and teachers. My desire is to accomplish everything You have called me to do in ministry. I thank You for the spiritual leader that You have given me. I pray that my spiritual leader will maintain a vigilant eye, watching and praying for me. I submit to the leader that You have placed over me. I pray that my leader will work with me to help me develop the ministry gifts that You have placed in me. Help me to remain humble and obedient to those You have

placed as teachers, mentors, and coaches for me.
I pray for clarity and understanding so that I
may be able to use the gifts to Your glory.

I realize that as I walk with You, I will
continue to develop and mature in You. Help
me to understand the seriousness of what You
have called me to do so that I do not take it
lightly. I realize that teachers will be held
accountable, and I am committed to not lead
any of Your children astray.

Grant me boldness to speak the truth. Do
not let me look at the faces of the people and
experience fear. But I stand in faith knowing
that what You have deposited in me, through
Your strength I am well able to deliver it.

I pray for the relationships that I have with
others. If I am connected to anyone that will not
help me in the cause that You have called me to,
please reveal it to me now so I can effectively
minister to those individuals. In my mission to
fulfill the call to ministry, I realize that some
relationships may have to be severed. Dear God,
I pray for Your love and Your wisdom to make
the decisions that need to be made in order for
me to do what You have called me to do. It is
my desire to surround myself with those who
will enrich the call of God for my life and who
will be there for me, to pray and cover me as
needed.

Thank You, God, for this privilege I have to
be able to impact the lives of others through
Your holy Word. I commit my life to You
now and forever as a minister of the Gospel
of Jesus Christ. My pledge this day is to serve

You in every way possible. I realize that the call to ministry is not about me, but it is about accomplishing Your purpose on the earth. I make myself available for Your use today and every day. In Jesus' name I pray. Amen.

Servanthood

All believers are called to service somewhere within the local body. When an individual is called into ministry, that individual must understand what it means to serve. Ministry is about serving one another. John 12:26: "Whoever serves me must follow me; and where I am, my servant also will be. My Father will honor the one who serves me." Believers must follow the example of Jesus, one of self-sacrificing. Jesus came to serve not to be served. If we are to be like Him, then His example of servanthood is something that every believer should follow.

To be a self-sacrificing individual means that the needs of others take precedence. There are those who have been designated as servants within the local assembly. In the New Testament three words referring to deacons are used: *diakonos*, which means "servant"; *diakonia*, which means "service"; and *diakoneo*, which means "to serve."

Strong's Concordance gives the meaning of each of these words from the original language, Greek. Understanding the meaning and usage of each word will assist the reader in recognizing the roles of service in the New Testament church.

Strong's Concordance G1247: The verb *diakoneō* means to be a servant or an attendant, to wait or to host. This word speaks of women preparing food and other necessities of life to minister. Also to minister or serve using the office of a deacon.

Strong's Concordance G1248 gives the feminine noun which is *diakonia* which means attendance as a servant or aid, as in preparing and presenting food. It also refers to one who is of service, as in those who help meet needs by either the collecting or distributing of charities. *Diakonia* also refers to the office of the deacon in the church.

Strong's Concordance G1249 is the noun masculine/feminine *diakonos* meaning to run on errands, an attendant. *Diakonos* also refers to a waiter, as in waiting tables or other menial duties. One who, by virtue of the office assigned to him by the church, cares for the poor. The words deacon, minister, or servant are synonymous.

The Greek words used for deacon suggest many different kinds of service. The English word *deacon* also refers to many types of service. The feminine use of the word is *deaconess*, which means to serve in some capacity in aiding another.

These words are used around one hundred times in the New Testament, and they are usually interpreted with variations of the English words *serve* or *minister*. In John 2:5, 9: "His mother said to the servants, 'Do whatever he tells you'.... And the master of the banquet tasted the water that had been turned into wine. He did not realize where it had come from, though the servants who had drawn the water knew. Then he called the bridegroom aside." The word *servant* is from the Greek word *diakonos* (Strong's Concordance G1249). This Scripture refers to a particular form of service—those who serve tables, or waiters.

John 12:26: "Whoever serves me must follow me; and where I am, my servant also will be. My Father will honor the one who serves me" (Strong G1247 serve and G1249 servant). Here, no particular form of service is mentioned; this would refer to various forms of service.

In Acts 6:1-4: "In those days when the number of disciples was increasing, the Hellenistic Jews among them complained against the Hebraic Jews because their widows were being overlooked in the daily distribution of food. So the Twelve gathered all the disciples together and said, 'It would not be right for us to neglect the ministry of the word of God in order to wait on tables. Brothers and sisters, choose seven men from among you who are known to be full of the Spirit and wisdom. We will turn this responsibility over to them and will give our attention to prayer and the ministry of the word.'" The words *serve tables* in the KJV notes the word *serve* is *diakoneō* (Strong's Concordance G1247). The congregation was given the task of selecting men full of the Holy Ghost to serve in this area. In the New Testament times, trade was handled over tables. The work of governing and dispensing care to those in need would have been carried out over tables. This was a ministry of service. The word ministry in verse four translates *diakonia* (Strong's Concordance G1248).

While it is true that God has called all believers to the office of service, it is imperative that one's heart be right. It is important to select those who have an honest character to serve. Paul listed some personal qualifications. First, deacons must be men of dignity. First Timothy 3:8: "In the same way, deacons are to be worthy of respect, sincere, not indulging in much wine, and not pursuing dishonest gain."

Deacons fill a much needed leadership position in the local church. The men listed in Acts 6 seem to be the forerunners of this office and ministry. Acts 6:5-7: "This proposal pleased the whole group. They chose Stephen, a man full of faith and of the Holy Spirit; also Philip, Procorus, Nicanor, Timon, Parmenas, and Nicolas from Antioch, a convert to Judaism. They presented these men to the apostles, who prayed and laid their hands on them. So the word of God spread. The number of disciples in Jerusalem increased rapidly, and a large number of priests became obedient to the faith."

The men chosen had to be worthy of respect. They needed to be serious-minded men. The Greek word for "grave" is *semnos* (Strong's Concordance G4586) which means "venerable, honorable, reputable, serious, and stately." The same Greek word appears in Titus

2:2, which says that older men are to be "sober, grave, temperate, sound in faith, in charity, in patience." (KJV)

A servant must not be one who gossips. A servant must be consistent and righteous in what they say. Their word has to mean something more than just words coming from their mouths. The servant must be willing to stand behind the words that he speaks. The servant must not be addicted to wine. He must be able to think clearly, and wine can cloud one's thinking. He must also be able to handle money, demonstrating self-control in every area of his life. For if the servant has difficulty managing his own house, how will he be able to serve in the house of God?

Paul also listed some spiritual qualifications in 1 Timothy 3:9-13: "They must keep hold of the deep truths of the faith with a clear conscience. They must first be tested; and then if there is nothing against them, let them serve as deacons. In the same way, the women are to be worthy of respect, not malicious talkers but temperate and trustworthy in everything. A deacon must be faithful to his wife and must manage his children and his household well. Those who have served well gain an excellent standing and great assurance in their faith in Christ Jesus."

A deacon must have convictions based on the knowledge of true biblical doctrine. His clear conscience suggests that he lives out his principles. He must embrace the faith and relate the truth in his life. He must have a thriving relationship with his own family.

Those elected to serve must also first be tested; before one is officially appointed as a deacon, he must have proved himself faithful in serving the Lord. He must have proved himself to be committed and faithful. If a man has not been faithful over a small thing, then how can God trust him with larger things? If a person has not been faithful to serve in the local assembly, how can the leadership of the ministry have confidence that they will faithfully serve in the office of a deacon?

The servant must be ethically pure in every way, just as an elder is to be. Those who are not above accusation are disqualified from serving as deacons. In verse twelve, Paul writes, "Let deacons be husbands of only one wife," which also implies that deacons are to be morally pure. The main point is that a deacon must be totally consecrated and devoted to his wife. One can tell a lot about the faithfulness of an individual by how that individual relates to his immediate family. His faithfulness needs to be demonstrated in the home before being called to serve outside of the home.

Deacons are to be good managers of their children and their own households. A deacon must demonstrate management ability. The proving ground for leadership is how a man manages his children and household.

In light of women called to serve the Word of God, 1 Timothy 3:11 begins, "Women must likewise be dignified." Paul lays out what the wife of the deacon must be. These are excellent qualifications to look at when appointing women to the office of deaconess. The woman who functions in the office of a deaconess must not be a gossiper. She must not bear false accusations or slander. She must be temperate, abstaining from wine, and faithful in everything she does. She must be faithful in the transaction of business and the discharge of her official duties.

In Romans 16:1 Paul writes, "I commend to you our sister Phoebe, who is a servant of the church which is at Cenchrea." Phoebe was recognized by the church for her service. It is possible that she served in an official capacity as a deaconess at the church in Cenchrea.

Both men and women should be proven servants of Christ. Matthew 20:26-28: "Not so with you. Instead, whoever wants to become great among you must be your servant, and whoever wants to be first must be your slave— just as the Son of Man did not come to be served, but to serve, and to give his life as a ransom for many." Matthew 20:28: "Even as the Son of man came not to be ministered unto but to minister, and to give his life a ransom for many" (KJV). The word *minister* is *diakoneō* in the Greek. The measure of a great woman is not her status or influence but her ability to serve.

New Testament women who served would prepare the food and serve in other domestic capacities. These servants were to relieve others' necessities, for example to collect alms and distribute what was necessary to sustain life. They would take care of the poor and the sick. In most churches today these chores are delegated to the deacon or deaconess.

The term *diakoneo* is referred to in Scripture many times. Examples would be administered, administration, cared, contributing, support, serving, employ, in serving, minster, ministered, ministering, servant, serve, serve as deacons, served, served as deacons, serves, services rendered, serving, take care, wait, and waited.

Before a believer delves into the areas of service that she is called to, she must first understand not only what she has been called to do, but also have a full understanding of submission and how this action defines her success in service. Submission is paramount if one is to be effective in the area of services. Serving means putting others before ourselves. In addition, because we are created with such a forceful drive to appease our flesh, even our flesh will need to come under submission. The bottom line is that our will is not our own, but to do the will of Him who has called us to serve.

Because Jesus was the ultimate servant, we too should strive to be like Him as an example to others. Therefore, receiving the call to serve should demand nothing less than excellence. If one is to serve in excellence, this means having a spirit that is ready, willing, and available. Ready, because you have prepared yourself; willing, because you have acknowledged your call; and available, because you understand that everything you do is for the kingdom of God.

Those who have been called to serve must understand that the excellence of the call comes from God. Yes, strive and persevere, but understand that God is excellent, and He will give you what is needed to serve with excellence. We are called to serve because we are called to follow. Jesus said follow me. If we follow the ministry of Jesus, we see Him serving the needs of all that He encountered. Jesus is the ultimate demonstration of servanthood. He served his disciples, the woman with the issue of blood, the blind beggar, and others we read about in the Scriptures. In the Old Testament Moses, was called to serve. He served God and was charged with the mission of leading the Children of Israel out of Egypt. Moses is an example of being a servant of the Lord. David, Solomon, Elijah, and Jonah are all referred to as "His Servant." The commonality is that they received the call and followed.

Ephesians 2:10: "For we are God's handiwork, created in Christ Jesus to do good works, which God prepared in advance for us to do." Whenever you serve others in any way, you are actually serving God. You were saved so that you could do His holy work.

The call to serve requires following Jesus. He is our best example of servanthood. The call to serve requires being attentive to the needs of others, healing, proclaiming, teaching, and ministering. Serving requires doing the Father's will. Jesus is the epitome of what it means to serve. As believers, this is why we were called to serve, to follow the example of our Savior.

After Joseph's brothers sold him into Egypt and during the time of famine, his brothers came for food. Joseph tested his brothers' character by having his servants place his brothers' money in their bags and his silver cup in Benjamin's bag. The brothers offered to give whoever had the silver cup as a servant to Joseph. Once they discovered the silver cup in Benjamin's sack, they despaired. Genesis 44:10: "'Very well, then,' he said, 'let it be as you say. Whoever is found to have it will become my slave; the rest of you will be free from blame.'"

Mark 9:35: "Sitting down, Jesus called the Twelve and said, 'Anyone who wants to be first must be the very last, and the servant of all.'"

These scriptures in Genesis and Mark sum up what it means to be a good servant. Genesis speaks of our character and Mark of our position. The term *servant* or *bond slave* is often used by men of God, such as Paul, to describe his total dedication to the cause of Christ. Romans 1:1: "Paul, a servant of Christ Jesus, called to be an apostle and set apart for the gospel of God." Paul is speaking of a servitude accepted willingly out of love, not the forced slavery.

Such submission to Christ is noted again in Romans 12:1: "Therefore, I urge you, brothers and sisters, in view of God's mercy, to offer your bodies as a living sacrifice, holy and pleasing to God—this is your true and proper worship." The King James Version calls it our "reasonable service." A good servant will understand that God requires us to give our best. This is our reasonable service. Understanding what is required of us should not deter the servant of God, but cause us to develop our character so that we can strive to lead a blameless life and work in the position in which we have been called to serve.

The faithful servant of God needs to understand the demands that will be placed on them and their families. We will talk more about the demands on the families later. Today we have been given many resources to prepare for our purpose. While it is vital to study and seek a deeper understanding of the Word in preparation for service, it is also equally as important to spend time in prayer. There is no substitute for spending time with the Father. This means seeking Him through prayer and fasting.

A committed servant surrenders her heart and mind totally to the Lord. Acts 2:18: "Even on my servants, both men and women, I will pour out my Spirit in those days, and they will prophesy." God will equip you with what you need to serve in His kingdom. Therefore, when the Holy Spirit comes upon you, understand God is giving you power, wisdom, and His Word. As He pours out His Spirit upon you, be willing to minister in whatever capacity is needed.

There will be many demands placed on you as a servant, as well as on your family. The main demand is one of time. This is why developing a time management plan is vital. To serve with excellence and still enjoy the blessings of this life requires balance and discipline. Balancing your time means defining your priorities. But what do you do when the Pastor calls a leader's meeting the same evening your child is being inducted into the National Honors Society at her school? How do you keep your lawn looking good and up to the Home Owner's Association standard? Work, caring for loved ones, planning meals, exercise, friends, vacation, balancing your life means defining your priorities. Everything you do needs to incorporate your love toward God. Learning to balance will be critical to your success in the call to serve.

A call to serve requires a committed individual, one who agrees to be faithful to God and to those they have been called to serve. God will equip individuals who have committed their lives to one of service. As you pray, allow God to reveal to you the people in your life that can assist you, and in return, you can assist them. Communicate with your family the area of service you have chosen and the importance of what you desire to do for Christ.

If you have been called to a service role within your local ministry and have to be absent from your post of servanthood due to family or work responsibilities, give advanced notification of your absence. Be willing to share your calendar of events with those with whom you serve. This will keep open the lines of communication and help your pastor or church leader. Early communication will also allow those in charge to find someone to fill in for you. Never take for granted the awesome privilege you have been given to serve the people of God. Many will be drawn to the kingdom by the love you show in your service.

Those willing to serve are most valuable to the work of ministry. By serving in ministry, you free up the leader to devote more time to the priorities of prayer and the ministry of the Word to those God has called him to serve.

> Blessed are the poor in spirit,
> for theirs is the kingdom of heaven.
> Blessed are those who mourn,
> for they will be comforted.
> Blessed are the meek,
> for they will inherit the earth.
> Blessed are those who hunger and thirst for
> righteousness,

for they will be filled.
Blessed are the merciful,
for they will be shown mercy.
Blessed are the pure in heart,
for they will see God.
Blessed are the peacemakers,
for they will be called sons of God.
Blessed are those who are persecuted because of righteousness, for theirs is the kingdom of heaven. Blessed are you when people insult you, persecute you and falsely say all kinds of evil against you because of me. Rejoice and be glad, because great is your reward in heaven, for in the same way they persecuted the prophets who were before you.

Matthew 5:3-12

A Servant's Prayer

Dear Heavenly Father

I give my life as one of service, first of all to You. Help me to follow Your example of what it truly means to be a servant. Your Word declares how You came into the world to seek, to save, and to serve mankind.

I desire to serve others. Give me the love and compassion that I will need to serve. I realize that sometimes the task before me may be difficult, but I also realize that I can do all things through You because You will strengthen me in the areas in which I need to be strengthened.

I pray that my family will be understanding and supportive of what You have called me to do. Help me not to take them for granted. Teach me how to manage my time so that my life can have balance. As I step out in the call that I believe You have for my life, help me to remain faithful over the small assignments that You have given me. Teach me how to use my life as an example of servanthood as I go about serving. Whatever my hands find to do, help me to do it with love. As You grant me Your grace and mercy for the journey ahead, I commit my life as a servant to the One who has saved me. Lord, help me to be faithful in what I have been called to do. I will extend myself to those I come in contact with in order to show the love of God through my service to others. In Jesus' name I pray. Amen.

Entrepreneurship

Although this is not a universal call to all women, there are those who find themselves being pulled in this direction. Many women have turned what started as a passion into a profitable business. If you believe God is calling you in the direction of starting your own business, this chapter will cover some very important material. I will cover information that will be valuable in assisting you to structure a business that will honor God.

An entrepreneur is one who organizes a new business endeavor with the expectation of making an income. Entrepreneurship is the method of collecting and distributing the means—monetary, innovative, decision-making, or scientific—necessary for a new project's achievement.

Some have been called by God to start their own business, but fear holds them back. While you are trying to fit into a job, God has called you to start your own business. You may not understand why you got laid off. You came to work early, and you remained late. You never missed a day, but you got a pink slip anyway. Well has God placed entrepreneurship in your heart and you have been hesitant to act on what He has said? Maybe you needed a tiny nudge, and the pink slip is what you needed to encourage you to move forward in your calling. Many times individuals get too comfortable where they are. So comfortable that they do not want to change anything. Being uncomfortable will stimulate people to change something in their lives.

Habakkuk 2:2-3: "Then the Lord replied: 'Write down the revelation and make it plain on tablets so that a herald may run with it. For the revelation awaits an appointed time; it speaks of the end and will not prove false. Though it linger, wait for it; it will certainly come and will not delay.'"

The prophet Habakkuk was instructed by God to position himself as a guard to look at the nations. Habakkuk waited with expectancy to see what God's answer would be to his criticisms noted in Habakkuk 1:12-17.

> LORD, are you not from everlasting? My God, my Holy One, you will never die. You, LORD, have appointed them to execute judgment; you, my Rock, have ordained them to punish. Your eyes are too pure to look on evil; you cannot tolerate wrongdoing. Why then do you tolerate

the treacherous? Why are you silent while the wicked swallow up those more righteous than themselves? You have made people like the fish in the sea, like the sea creatures that have no ruler. The wicked foe pulls all of them up with hooks, he catches them in his net, he gathers them up in his dragnet; and so he rejoices and is glad. Therefore he sacrifices to his net and burns incense to his dragnet, for by his net he lives in luxury and enjoys the choicest food. Is he to keep on emptying his net, destroying nations without mercy?

Habakkuk was questioning how God could permit the shameless actions of the Babylonians to continue. The prophet accused God of reducing humans to the level of fish or insects, causing confusion among the lands. The prophet's rational thoughts were that God must have had a need to chastise the Babylonians for their arrogance.

As Habakkuk stands in faith waiting for God's reaction, he is commanded to write the vision. This seems unusual to the prophet because normally prophets spoke the word of the Lord first. The term *vision* (used in the KJV) relates to the verb translated *saw* (Habakkuk 1:1) "The burden which the prophet Habakkuk saw" (NKJV). An appointed time speaks of a preset time as determined by God. When an individual is getting ready to go into the direction of entrepreneurship, that individual must be mindful that God moves on His own time. Many times people will want God to act on their timetable, but God has His own perfect time to make things happen.

God knows His strategy and the outcome of all things in agreement with His purposes. As believers our responsibility is to prepare and master our craft while waiting for the fulfillment of what God has placed in our heart. One good way to use the period of waiting is to prepare. Many times the reason we have to wait is because more time needs to be applied to preparation.

The Word of God says, "it will surely come." We have God's assurance of achieving the plan He has for us. The success of the vision comes from God, and it will not take any longer than God has planned. If an individual has prepared himself, when God is ready to open the door, that individual can become productive, immediately eliminating the struggles that the unprepared person will encounter.

All large businesses started out small, usually by one man or one woman who had a good idea and was willing to put forth the necessary effort. If an individual believes God is leading them to start their own business, this is an honorable goal. Not only will it be beneficial to that individual, but it can also lead to employment for others.

What a great way for God to use you to bless His people by putting you in a position to offer someone employment. Growing a business requires much hard work. Dedication and research will be necessary. If you have no business experience or business education, it will be essential for you to seek out the counsel of someone who can guide you on how to write a good business plan.

Remember, Habakkuk was told by God to write the vision and make it plain. It is very easy to speak things regarding what one wants to do out of the mouth, but a serious person will write it down. Putting your ideas on paper is very important. When you write the vision, not only do you see it before you, but others can see it as well. If it is in your mind only, no one else can see it. There is something about writing it that makes it seem possible. When one writes things down, they become more real. Not only that, but now others can see the vision when it is written.

Seek out a mentor who can assist you with this undertaking. A mentor will be able to advise you and hold you accountable. Having someone to talk things over with can make a big difference. Having someone to pray with you regarding your decision can bring clarity as to what you are to accomplish. It is so important to have an ear just to bounce ideas off of.

As you pursue your calling to start your own business, it is imperative not to miss any crucial stages. Skipping essential stages will most likely cause you problems down the road. Why not just get it right the first time so that you will not have to repeat it.

Before you start your business, training most likely will be required even if you have experience it that particular area. The art of being prepared can never be underestimated. Taking classes on how to start a business, even if they are online classes, will be beneficial. Attend workshops and seminars on how to start a business. An entrepreneur can never have too much information on hand regarding their vision for their business. The process of preparation should not be undervalued.

Some businesses start out as home-based businesses, but not everyone will enjoy working from home. There are many things that you will need to consider before starting a home-based business. Is your home set up in such a way that a home-based business can be accommodated? Does the home allow space that can be designated only for the business? How will this home-based business influence your family's current living arrangements? If the business is to be customer based, do you want strangers coming in and out of your home? Do you have the discipline to shut everything down at the designated time if you are working from home? These are just a few questions to consider.

Operating a business from your home may require modification being done to the home, so the cost of the renovations will need to be considered in the financial planning of the startup cost. Also, depending on where you live, your neighbors may be disrupted by you running a home-based business. Parking may be an issue, and your community may have restrictions on operating a home-based business. All of these things will need to be checked out during the preparation phase.

For the Christian entrepreneur, there may be temptation at times to make a decision based on what is profitable. Anytime the decision requires something that is unethical, the Christian entrepreneur must follow biblical principles. A Christian business cannot be conducted the same as a secular business. God will hold you accountable for how you run your business.

The Christian business owner must show that she is trustworthy. It is an instinct for people not to trust business owners. It has been said that it is all about making money. With the Christian entrepreneur, revenue cannot be the bottom line. When we serve people, whether it is customers or parishioners, we must do it as unto God. The Christian business owner's character must remain intact at all cost.

When someone feels they cannot trust you as a business owner, they will go somewhere else. When a business loses too many customers it will eventually have to go out of business. So not only does the owner have to be driven by strong ethics, but all of those who work in the business must have the same strong ethics as the owner.

It is not wise for the Christian to go into business with a nonbeliever. The nonbeliever will not possess the same godly principles that you live by. Second Corinthians 6:14: "Do not be yoked together with unbelievers. For what do righteousness and wickedness have in common? Or what fellowship can light have with darkness?"

This Scripture is used many times when discussing marriage, but it can also apply in choosing a business partner. Make sure your business partner has similar work ethics.

Amos 3:3: "Do two walk together unless they have agreed to do so?" The answer to the question is no. It is not a wise decision to have a nonbelieving business partner if you are a Christian. When it comes to giving the tenth from your business profits, the nonbeliever may disagree with you. If you want your business to be blessed, then you must honor God in all that you do. The Bible teaches that two cannot walk together unless they agree. Nonbelievers and Christians will not agree. When a tough decision has to be made, it should be made after much prayer.

A Christian who decides to go into business must have a strong character. Integrity is needed to be an entrepreneur. Many situations will arise that will require the business owner to make difficult decisions necessitating honesty and integrity. Some decisions may mean a forfeiture of profit, but the Christian business owner must stand on the Word of God even in running a business.

Having a successful business requires a strong work ethic and commitment to the consumer. If the business is scheduled to open at 9:00 each morning, the doors cannot open at 9:05. And if the business is scheduled to close at 5:00 p.m. you cannot close at 4:59 p.m. The customer needs to know they can trust what you say even regarding opening and closing times. They need to know that you will be there when they need the service you are offering.

Planning is very important in having a thriving business. Will you have enough staff to relieve you when you have to take time off? Emergencies happen, and you will need time off for relaxation. One of the challenges a new business faces is the owner working nonstop because she cannot afford to hire help.

Remember, you want whatever you do to bring glory to God, including running your business. God will take no glory in you suffering burnout and fatigue because you are understaffed. It may take some years before an entrepreneur starts to see a financial profit, but if this is an area you believe God has called you to, stay the course. Many times people feel passion about something and start moving toward their goals. But when things do not happen as quickly as they would like, they give up. They sometimes give up right before the harvest.

Ecclesiastes 9:11: "I have seen something else under the sun: The race is not to the swift or the battle to the strong, nor does food come to the wise or wealth to the brilliant or favor to the learned; but time and chance happen to them all."

Ecclesiastes 9:11: "I returned, and saw under the sun, that the race is not to the swift, nor the battle to the strong, neither yet bread to the wise, nor yet riches to men of understanding, nor yet favor to men of skill; but time and chance happeneth to them all" (ASV).

Do your research before starting your business. Check your motives. What are you trying to accomplish? See if what you are trying to accomplish is something that is needed. Passion is good, but there has to be a market for your product. If the market is not there, you will not be successful. Yes, God honors faithfulness, but you need to give God something to work with. Do your research. Know what is needed in the market. Beware of the times and the changes that are going on in the world. I am an author and I enjoy writing inspirational nonfiction books, but I am keenly aware that technology has made it necessary to have my books available electronically if I want to be successful.

Evaluate what it is you are passionate about. If you have a passion for something, perhaps what you have is a hobby and not necessarily a business venture. Your passion is something that you would do if no profits were involved, but this is different than having a successful business. That is not to say that your passion cannot turn into a successful business, because it can. But if it is truly something that you enjoy doing and you would do it for free, by all means do not give it up, but be prepared to do it for free for a long time.

The market has to support the business you are starting if you desire to make a profit. I really believe there is a market for most things; you just have to find it. You may have to reach outside your comfort zone and start the business in another neighborhood or another state.

An example would be that if I design snow sleds, then living in Florida is probably not the best place for me. But if I worked hard enough, I could most likely have a successful business with contracts outside of the state that I live in. It would take a little more planning on my part as the business owner, but it can be done. The owner would need to be ready to ship the merchandise rather than have customers walk in off the streets of sunny Florida asking for snow sleds.

Do research in the area of finances, as well, to see what funding may be available to you. There may be start-up funds available to start small businesses. There also may be grant money available if you are starting a not-for-profit business. Please note that a not-for-profit business does not mean you do not make profit. Although you cannot personally create a profit from starting a nonprofit, the nonprofit can create a job doing meaningful and exciting work that you enjoy, thereby generating an income for you.

If you have to borrow money to start your business, only borrow what is necessary to start. Some needs, such as decorative furniture, can be delayed. Borrow as little as possible to get your business started. Remember to pay the money back as soon as you can.

Mothers who want to be at home with their children, but because of finances are prohibited, may start a home daycare. While caring for other children, a mother will be able to spend quality time with her own. She will be able to pour into the lives of other precious little ones while teaching her own children. This would be a great help to many mothers who are looking for a safe, godly environment to leave their children.

Women who love doing hair may open a salon and find fulfillment in providing spiritual encouragement to their clients while doing their hair. The hair stylist will come in contact with many women during the course of the day. She will be able to speak the Word of God to those who may otherwise not hear it. What a privilege to have a business that will allow you to speak into the lives of hurting women.

Someone who is very creative may open a florist shop or art gallery and use her talent to brighten the lives of seniors. She can volunteer her time to teach classes in medical facilities and work with children. Any gift that God has given can be used to build up people and encourage them. This is a rewarding business as the beauty of flowers and art will bring joy to many while generating an income for the family.

A gifted musician may offer music lessons as a business opportunity for herself, but also offer her services as a volunteer to comfort those who are sick in hospitals. During the course of my husband's illness and frequent hospitalizations, we have enjoyed the soothing music of many musicians. When a musician owns her own business, she will have the flexibility to donate hours to bring joy to those in pain. The smiles that come as a result of music are amazing.

There are many things that women can do to generate income while being of service to others. Whatever gift or talent God has blessed you with, He can use it to provide resources for you and your family. Never underestimate what God will use you to do to bless His people. Service is to be extended beyond the church walls.

If you believe God has gifted you in a certain area and you want to pursue it as a business opportunity, do not be afraid. Seek God for direction and ask Him to put the right people in your path. Everyone has been given something from God; however it is up to each person to move forward and use what God has given.

Starting a business can be very difficult, but if you believe this is something that God has called you to do, work hard. If you put forth the hard work required, God will bless your efforts, and you can become a successful Christian entrepreneur.

Keep a positive attitude; if you feel your attitude leaning toward negativity, go into prayer. Complaining will not change the course of your business, but hard work accompanied with prayer can make all the difference in the world.

In the beginning, God created the heavens and the earth, so I am sure God has no objections to you owning your own business. Just remember to build your business on biblical principles and watch God prosper your business. I have included some inspiring Scripture for future or current business owners

> The LORD God took the man and put him in the Garden of Eden to work it and take care of it.
>
> Genesis 2:15

> But if from there you seek the LORD your God, you will find him if you seek him with all your heart and with all your soul.
>
> Deuteronomy 4:29

> Why, my soul, are you downcast? Why so disturbed within me? Put your hope in God, for I will yet praise him, my Savior and my God.
>
> Psalm 42:5

Unless the LORD builds the house, the builders labor in vain. Unless the LORD watches over the city, the guards stand watch in vain.

Psalm 127:1

Plans fail for lack of counsel, but with many advisers they succeed.

Proverbs 15:22

Commit to the LORD whatever you do, and he will establish your plans.

Proverbs 16:3

The plans of the diligent lead to profit as surely as haste leads to poverty.

Proverbs 21:5

Pride brings a person low, but the lowly in spirit gain honor.

Proverbs 29:23

Give, and it will be given to you. A good measure, pressed down, shaken together and running over, will be poured into your lap. For with the measure you use, it will be measured to you.

Luke 6:38

By myself I can do nothing; I judge only as I hear, and my judgment is just, for I seek not to please myself but him who sent me.

John 5:30

I am the vine; you are the branches. If you remain in me and I in you, you will bear much fruit; apart from me you can do nothing.

John 15:5

Therefore, I urge you, brothers and sisters, in view of God's mercy, to offer your bodies as a living sacrifice, holy and pleasing to God—this is your true and proper worship. Do not conform to the pattern of this world, but be transformed by the renewing of your mind. Then you will be able to test and approve what God's will is—his good, pleasing and perfect will.

Romans 12:1-2

For we live by faith, not by sight.

2 Corinthians 5:7

Do not be deceived: God cannot be mocked. A man reaps what he sows.

Galatians 6:7

However, as it is written: "What no eye has seen, what no ear has heard, and what no human mind has conceived" the things God has prepared for those who love him."

1 Corinthians 2:9

An Entrepreneur's Prayer

Dear Heavenly Father

I believe that You have called me to start my own business. Please direct my path as I pursue what You have placed in my heart. Help me to lean not on my own understanding but to acknowledge You in all my ways. As I write the vision You have placed in my heart, allow me to see clearly the plan that You have for me. I want to honor You in all I do, even with this business plan. Help me to seek out wise counsel that I may know the direction You would have for me to take. I pledge to be faithful in my endeavors to build this business. I promise to give the tenth from all that I earn. I promise to keep the principles of Your Word at the center of my business. I pray for every customer that You will bless me with. I pray for the provisions that You have already made. Thank You for helping me to prepare myself for the challenges that lie ahead. I thank You for the people You have put in my path who will assist me as I walk out the call of God for my life. I thank You for the mentoring, the training, the encouragement, and the support that others will offer. Please keep my heart open and pure to receive what is offered, in the Spirit in which it is offered to me. Help me to not be judgmental, negative, or arrogant. My utmost desire is to bring glory and honor to Your name. I pray for a clean heart so that I may serve You in all that I do. Help me to seek You in any decisions that I make regarding a partner for my business. In Jesus' name I pray. Amen.

Passionate Pursuit

Many women live their whole lives with no direction, wandering aimlessly, wishing and hoping that they are going in the right direction. Women all over the world are hoping somehow they will happen to stumble onto the right path. If a woman does not know which way is right, how will she know when she has arrived at the right path? Fulfilling one's destiny is not about stumbling into it, but about seeking God for direction.

Many believe that their destiny is to be happy, make a lot of money, have a nice family, and travel the world. While all of these are good goals to aspire toward,

God's plan and purpose for one's life is so much deeper than that.

There is nothing wrong with enjoying life. But if one's complete purpose in life is to simply enjoy life, then may I suggest to you that is an empty life. There is no real substance to a life that is being lived merely for enjoyment. If we only do what makes us feel good, then we are simply satisfying the flesh.

Solomon wrote in the book of Ecclesiastes that God put "eternity in our hearts." Ecclesiastes 3:11: "He has made everything beautiful in its time. He has also set eternity in the human heart, yet no one can fathom what God has done from the beginning to end." We have a big God and that same big God has a big purpose for the lives of those who believe and trust Him.

Solomon examined the things that commonly motivate us in life.

> I said to myself, "Come now, I will test you with pleasure to find out what is good." But that also proved to be meaningless. "Laughter," I said, "is madness. And what does pleasure accomplish?" I tried cheering myself with wine, and embracing folly—my mind still guiding me with wisdom. I wanted to see what was good for people to do under the heavens during the few days of their lives. I undertook great projects: I built houses for myself and planted vineyards. I made gardens and parks and planted all kinds of fruit trees in them. I made reservoirs to water groves of flourishing trees. I bought male and female slaves and had other slaves who were born in my house. I also owned more herds and flocks

than anyone in Jerusalem before me. I amassed silver and gold for myself, and the treasure of kings and provinces. I acquired male and female singers and a harem as well—the delights of a man's heart. I became greater by far than anyone in Jerusalem before me. In all this my wisdom stayed with me. I denied myself nothing my eyes desired; I refused my heart no pleasure. My heart took delight in all my labor, and this was the reward for all my toil. Yet when I surveyed all that my hands had done and what I had toiled to achieve, everything was meaningless, a chasing after the wind; nothing was gained under the sun."

Ecclesiastes 2:1-11

What Solomon reminds us is that all the pleasures that life offers cannot compare to living a life of purpose. A life of purpose brings more pleasure than anything else in life. Living a life of purpose cannot be measured by riches or fame. A purposeful life brings a contentment that can only come from doing what God has created you to do. An individual may accomplish every dream but still lack purpose. One may pursue and achieve learning to the highest level, but without purpose it is meaningless. There are many powerful people in this world who are very unhappy. They hold high positions and have great riches but are living a meaningless life. Security is not a substitute for purpose. Learning, power, position, riches, and security—one can have it all, but if purpose is missing from the equation it means nothing.

After careful consideration, Solomon comes to a conclusion about what is important in life. When he finishes his evaluation of each ambition, he recognizes that it is all good but not fulfilling. Solomon declared that these things are not what is important. He said it is all empty, worthless, and dissatisfying.

A life without purpose and direction is useless. Solomon speaks of all of his projects, the houses he built, and the gardens he planted. He speaks of the slaves he owned, the herd, flock, riches, and having all the women he could desire. He said, "I refused my heart no pleasure." Think about what Solomon is saying here. For many people they can only imagine a life where no pleasure is off limits. But here we have a man that had experienced it all and he still said all of it was meaningless.

Friends, it does not matter how rich you are, how educated you are, and how successful you think you are. Money cannot buy your purpose. Many of the things we place great value on are temporary. God wants to put purpose in the heart of all believers. He wants to give you a reason for getting out of bed in the morning. God has a plan for your life. Why not seek Him for clarity on what He has called you to do?

There is another example in the New Testament nearly a thousand years after Solomon's evaluation. Let's look at what Paul wrote.

> But whatever were gains to me I now consider loss for the sake of Christ. What is more, I consider everything a loss because of the surpassing worth of knowing Christ Jesus my

Lord, for whose sake I have lost all things. I consider them garbage, that I may gain Christ and be found in him, not having a righteousness of my own that comes from the law, but that which is through faith in Christ—the righteousness that comes from God on the basis of faith. I want to know Christ—yes, to know the power of his resurrection and participation in his sufferings, becoming like him in his death, and so, somehow, attaining to the resurrection from the dead. Not that I have already obtained all this, or have already arrived at my goal, but I press on to take hold of that for which Christ Jesus took hold of me. Brothers and sisters, I do not consider myself yet to have taken hold of it. But one thing I do: Forgetting what is behind and straining toward what is ahead, I press on toward the goal to win the prize for which God has called me heavenward in Christ Jesus.

Philippians 3:7-14

Paul writes, "I want to know Christ so that I may be like Him." Simply put, Paul's reason for living was to be like Christ. Paul's desire was to have an intimate relationship with Christ. If one is to pursue with passion the call, that individual must have an intimate relationship with Christ.

Paul, like Solomon, had many things in his favor. He was a leader; people looked up to him. Paul had a bright future ahead of him. But Paul had come to the place where he understood that it was all rubbish, excess debris, worthless junk. Paul said, "I count all my successes as things worthless and detestable." It meant nothing to Paul to be educated or to be a leader. It no longer made him feel powerful to have people looking up to him. He had come to a place in his life where he realized that a relationship with Christ was the priority. Paul understood that his main focus had to be one of pursuit. When God called, Saul answered, and his name was later changed to Paul.

Friends, when you make a decision to pursue your purpose with passion, nothing matters except doing what God has called you to do. The things of God must take priority in the lives of His people. When one comes to know the Lord Jesus Christ as Savior and Lord, an evaluation must take place. It is no more about what we want to do. Instead we are seeking God for divine direction as to which path He would have us take. It is at this time our dialogue changes from asking what we want to asking God what His plan for our life is.

If the plan and purpose of God is to be fulfilled, one must follow the words of Paul. "Brethren, I count not myself to have apprehended: but this one thing I do, forgetting those things which are behind, and reaching forth unto those things which are before, I press toward the mark for the prize of the high calling of God in Christ Jesus." Philippians 3:13-14 (KJV)

To walk in destiny we need to forget the past. Those bad things in your past, Paul said to forget them. Paul, before his conversion, was named Saul. Like many believers today, he had a past that was best forgotten. Saul had tortured and murdered Christians and was on his way to continue his plan when God interrupted him.

Meanwhile, Saul was still breathing out murderous threats against the Lord's disciples. He went to the high priest and asked him for letters to the synagogues in Damascus, so that if he found any there who belonged to the Way, whether men or women, he might take them as prisoners to Jerusalem. As he neared Damascus on his journey, suddenly a light from heaven flashed around him. He fell to the ground and heard a voice say to him, "Saul, Saul, why do you persecute me?" "Who are you, Lord?" Saul asked. "I am Jesus, whom you are persecuting," he replied. "Now get up and go into the city, and you will be told what you must do." The men traveling with Saul stood there speechless; they heard the sound but did not see anyone. Saul got up from the ground, but when he opened his eyes he could see nothing. So they led him by the hand into Damascus. For three days he was blind, and did not eat or drink anything.

In Damascus there was a disciple named Ananias. The Lord called to him in a vision, "Ananias!" "Yes, Lord," he answered. The Lord told him, "Go to the house of Judas on Straight Street and ask for a man from Tarsus named Saul, for he is praying. In a vision he has seen a man named Ananias come and place his hands on him to restore his sight." "Lord," Ananias answered, "I have heard many reports about this man and all the harm he has done to your holy people in Jerusalem. And he has come here with authority from the chief priests to arrest all who call on your name."

Acts 9:1-13

Saul had caused a lot of pain and had done much damage to the cause of Christ. In Acts 9, he was wholeheartedly set to defend his Jewish faith from the new Jewish messianic sect. The letters he sought were documents authorizing him to arrest Christians in Damascus. Saul planned to take the Christians back to Jerusalem to stand trial and possibly face a death sentence.

Saul had an encounter with the Lord Jesus as he traveled along the road. The Lord would send Ananias to find Saul, the man who had persecuted the Christians. After Saul's conversion he had a choice to make. He could dwell on his past mistakes and let them ruin his life and his chance for real ministry, or he could forget all about the mistakes and pursue with passion the plan and purpose of God for his life.

Each individual has done something that they are not proud of. Many people get upset when someone brings up their past. Everyone has a story, some more remarkable than others, but a story nonetheless. Just as Paul did, each individual must decide to let the past remain in the past and move toward fulfilling the call of God for their life.

Paul had to make a choice; so do we. Maybe you have done something you are ashamed of, and you still have regrets. Maybe the memories keep coming back to haunt you and keep you from living a full life today. Every time you try to move forward, the memories of what you have done stop you. When you try to pursue your call with passion, others will not let you forget things you have done in your past. You may have regrets. We all have some regrets, but we must forget the past! Many people will say, "I just cannot forgive myself." Jesus went to the cross for your sins. He is the only one who can forgive sin. He took care of that when He shed His blood on the cross. Our duty is to receive the forgiveness that He died to give to us. If one has confessed their sins, then that individual's sins have been forgiven. The person that God has forgiven can move into purpose by beginning to walk in the plan of God for her life.

The past cannot be changed. The only productive thing to do is to forget and move on. God has a plan for your life, and you will never walk in your destiny as long as you are holding on to the past. Holding on to the past will slow you down and will hinder you from fulfilling the call of God for your life. Let it go!

If you want to fulfill your purpose, you have to forget the past, leave the garbage in the garbage can, and move into your destiny. Do not continue rehashing over and over what you used to do. The Bible teaches in 2 Corinthians 5:17 that if any man is in Christ, he is a new creation and that old things are passed away. You have been restored to what God originally created you to be. All things have become new. When one receives Jesus by faith, that individual's life is transformed into the likeness of Christ. Instead of living the way you used to live, you live the way Christ wants you to live. So if I am new, then I am not that person anymore. Therefore, I do not need to bring up what I used to do because that is not my reality now that I am in Christ. Not only is it not my reality, but that past is no longer applicable to me. That was the old me. I am a new creation now, so I now live for Christ.

When you make up your mind to pursue your purpose, it is vital that you understand that the junk of the past will try to hold you hostage. You will not be able to take junk with you as you passionately pursue your destiny. Destiny-driven people do not have time to hang out gossiping about other people. There is no room for jealousy on the road to pursuing one's destiny.

A purpose-driven individual must separate from negativity and anything else that removes her focus from where she is headed. A destiny-driven person cannot dwell on the haters. Sometimes people will not understand or appreciate what you are trying to achieve. Some will not like you just because. If you desire to pursue your purpose, then you must forget the haters and move toward purpose and destiny. Someone may have done you wrong, and yes, that is a bad thing, but you will need to release that person so that you can move on. It may be especially difficult when it is someone close to you, but many times people who are close to you will not appreciate the journey you are on. It may cost you some relationships if you want to achieve your goals. As one begins to move away from one's past, there are some people that will need to be left in the past. Sadly, those who have been close may try to sabotage the path that destiny-driven people pursue. Often the attempt to sabotage is not on purpose; they just do not know any better. There will be others who will attempt to sabotage your journey on purpose because they do not want you to succeed.

A change in environment may be necessary if one is serious about pursuing the call of God. It will not be profitable to visit some of the old places you used to hang around with the old memories. Being new in Christ means that new memories will need to be made of a Christ-centered life. God has a plan for the lives of those who will yield themselves to Him. The plan that God has may not include some of the people that one's flesh wishes to bring along. If you want to fulfill the call of God for your life, you will need to keep company with like-minded people.

Many individuals like to focus on a good period in their lives and spend each day trying to relive the past. Some people are stuck in college, the good old days, and never want to grow up. Even in the church, we have the good-old-days mentality. Many will reminisce about how it was a long time ago, who used to be here, or what office was held by certain people. It does us no good to have started walking in the plan of God for our lives and stall by the wayside. The most important thing is what one is doing in the present. How are people who love God using their gifts and talents today to bring glory to Him?

Paul knew that a good past was not enough to guarantee a meaningful future. He writes about being able to trace his roots back to the tribe of Benjamin, the tribe that produced the first king of Israel and was loyal to David. Paul wanted to demonstrate to these Jews that he had earned the right to speak. He was not only an Israelite; he belonged to the select of Israel. Paul went on to share regarding the fact that he was of the tribe that joined Judah after the exile, the one that helped restore the nation. Paul was educated as a Jew. He was a trained Pharisee. He is not judging Judaism from the outside. He had experienced it all, and he knew that it was naught equated with the joy which Christ had given. Paul understood that the only way to fulfill the plan of God for his life was to accept the grace. Paul was highly educated, but he realized that these things did not matter in relationship to what God had called him to do.

Paul points out, "I will not live in the past. My reason for living is to be like Christ, and whatever happened yesterday, good or bad, is now ancient history. I will live my life with purpose. Since the Lord stopped me on the road to Damascus, my priorities have changed. The things I considered unimportant are now important to me. I am a citizen of the kingdom, so I have a kingdom mind-set." Paul was now a citizen of the kingdom and citizens of the kingdom have the mind of Christ.

All believers have their own story to tell about their past, their encounter with Christ, and about what event drew them to Christ. Each person has a testimony regarding the "old you." God will use that testimony to draw others to Him, but He does not want you using your testimony as an excuse for not pursuing His call for your life. Just because a person has failed, does not mean that person has to keep repeating the mistakes of her past.

The world has many eye-pleasing things to offer. Many people are in pursuit of worldly treasures and worldly accomplishments. Learn from Solomon, who found that none of those things made life worth living. Those who chase after money will soon find out that money will not make them happy. The pursuit of fame or the approval of man will not bring true fulfillment. It is one's chase, hunger, and passion for the things of God that places the believer in the position to pursue God's plan for their life.

The things of our past, however significant they may be, are small compared to what God has in store for those who love and trust Him. God is more concerned with our future than with our past.

Which direction are you heading? Are you heading toward the plan of God for your life or the plan that you have for your life? It matters less what is behind us and most what is before us. Messed up? We all have, but our God is able to turn any situation around. Scripture teaches that when we confess our sins, God will forgive us.

First John 1:9: "If we confess our sins, he is faithful and just and will forgive us our sins and purify us from all unrighteousness."

God does not need to probe your past to decide your future. He knew you even before you were formed in your mother's womb. God spoke to the Prophet Jeremiah in Jeremiah 1:5: "Before I formed you in the womb I knew you, before you were born I set you apart; I appointed you as a prophet to the nations." Jeremiah was profoundly conscious of the fact that the call of God in his life had been decided by God from before the time of his conception.

As God's Word became truth in his life, the prophet agreed that God knew him and had called him to declare a serious message at a vital time in the history of the nation. The word *knew* comes from the Hebrew word *yada* (Strong's Concordance H3045) meaning to perceive and see, find out and discern to discriminate, or to distinguish. This word *know* also refers to know by experience, to recognize, admit, acknowledge, confess to consider, and to be acquainted with. Jeremiah 1:5 refers to the intimate familiarity that comes from relationship and personal commitment. That intimate relationship was made apparent in God's sanctifying work, whereby Jeremiah was set apart for distinctive service. His calling was that of a prophet to the nations of Judah as well as a messenger of God for all nations.

In Ephesians 2:10 Paul writes, "We are His workmanship, created in Christ Jesus for good works that He prepared in advance for us to do." Workmanship comes from the Greek word *poiēma* (Strong's Concordance G4161) meaning that which has been made.

We have been made to do good works that He prepared in advance for us to do. The KJV Ephesians 2:10 reads, "For we are his workmanship, created in Christ Jesus unto good works, which God hath before ordained that we should walk in them." Notice the KJV uses the words *before ordained* which comes from the Greek word *proetoimazō* (Strong's Concordance G4282) meaning to prepare before, to make ready beforehand. We have an established destiny. Let me say it this way: you were created for a purpose. The purpose did not come later; God's plan for you was not an afterthought. When God created you He already knew what He would do with you.

An easy example to further clarify what I am saying is that it is similar to baking a cake. A baker does not bake a cake and say, "Oh, I have this cake. What shall I do with it?" The baker has a purpose for the cake before he bakes the cake. Whether it is a wedding or Sunday dinner, the cake was baked for a purpose. When God created you He already knew how and what He would use you for.

> For he chose us in him before the creation of the world to be holy and blameless in his sight. In love he predestined us for adoption to sonship through Jesus Christ, in accordance with his pleasure and will— to the praise of his glorious grace, which he has freely given us in the one he loves. In him we have redemption through his blood, the forgiveness of sins, in accordance with the riches of God's grace that he lavished on us. With all wisdom and understanding, he made known to us the mystery of his will according to his good pleasure, which he purposed in Christ, to be put into effect when the times reach their fulfillment—to bring unity to all things in heaven and on earth under Christ. In him we were also chosen, having been predestined according to the plan of him who works out everything in conformity with the purpose of his will, in order that we, who were the first to put our hope in Christ, might be for the praise of his glory.
>
> Ephesians 1:4-12

The KJV Ephesians 1:4 uses the word *foundation* instead of *creation*. *Foundation* comes from the Greek word *katabolē*, which means (Strong's Concordance G2602) conception, conceive. The injection or depositing of the virile semen in the womb. Before your mother and your father got together, God said (paraphrasing), "I already know you. I know what I am going to do with you; I know what I am going to do through you. I chose you." We did not choose God. He chose us before the foundation of the world. The word *chosen* means to pick out for oneself. This deals with God's divine plan of redemption for humankind.

God had already decided beforehand the purpose and plan for your life. Before mother knew father, God knew you. In Ephesians 1:5: Paul writes concerning the pleasure of His will. *Will* comes from the Greek word *thelēma* (Strong's Concordance G2307) meaning what one wishes or has determined shall be done, of the purpose of God to bless mankind through Christ, of what God wishes to be done by us. The word *will* also has to do with commands, precepts, choice, inclination, desire, and pleasure.

In Ephesians 1:9, Paul also writes concerning the good pleasures He has purposed in Himself. The word *purposed* in the Greek is *protithēmai* (Strong's Concordance G4388) meaning to place before, to set forth, to be looked at, expose to view, to purpose, determine. The mystery referred to in this verse is not a riddle to unravel, or to be understood only by a few chosen ones. Paul is referring to a characteristic of God's will that was once hidden but now has been shown or revealed by God.

The fact that God chose you before the foundation of the world was not a compassionless choice or a destiny of disaster. It was a decision made out of His great love for you. It was God's choice, His will, to love you. God made a decision to love us.

To passionately pursue one's purpose, the past cannot be a constant thought. God is not dwelling on your past, so why should you? Not even satan is threatened by your accomplishments of the past. He wants to derail your future, your purpose, and your destiny. His main goal is to stop you from fulfilling the call of God for your life.

It is imperative that each individual realizes that the things of this world will not last. No matter how good it is, it will not last. Pleasure, ever so sweet, will not last. Possessions, regardless of how many, will not last.

First Timothy 6:7 says, "For we brought nothing into the world, and we can take nothing out of it."

I used to hear my dad say, "I have conducted a lot of funerals in my lifetime as a pastor, but I have never seen a U-haul behind a hearse." What my dad was saying was that, regardless of your earthly abundance, you will not be able to take any of it with you when you leave this earth.

A good reputation is needed, but it will not matter in the great scheme of things. Jesus said in Matthew 20:16, "So the last will be first, and the first will be last." Many people whom we exalt as important will be the least important in eternity. Only what we do for Christ will count in eternity. The Scripture teaches that we should lay up treasures in heaven, not on earth.

Jesus said in Mark 8:36, "What good is it for a man to gain the whole world, yet forfeit his soul?" First John 2:17 tells us: "The world and its desires pass away, but the man who does the will of God lives forever."

Acts 5:28-30: "'We gave you strict orders not to teach in this name,' he said. 'Yet you have filled Jerusalem with your teaching and are determined to make us guilty of this man's blood.' Peter and the other apostles replied: 'We must obey God rather than human beings! The God of our ancestors raised Jesus from the dead—whom you killed by hanging him on a cross.'"

A true servant of the Lord seeks to obey in every way. Obedience to God is vital if we are to walk in the plan of God for our lives. Paul wrote, "Brothers and sisters, I do not consider myself yet to have taken hold of it. But one thing I do: Forgetting what is behind and straining toward what is ahead, I press on toward the goal to win the prize for which God has called me heavenward in Christ Jesus." Philippians 3:13-14. *Forgetting* comes from the Greek word *epilanthanomai* (Strong's Concordance G1950) meaning neglecting, no longer caring for, given over to oblivion, uncared for. If I am forgetting what is behind, that means that I do not care about that anymore. I have put it out of my mind, and those things behind me have no more power over me.

Yesterday's news is old news. We must keep our purpose at the forefront of everything we do. When we keep our purpose in view, we do not have time to be petty. Our purpose is bigger than the challenges that seek to take us off course. Minor infractions do not weary a purpose-driven individual. Purpose-driven individuals are not fazed by the snickers, the eye rolling, or the funny looks. Many disappointments may be in a person's history, but when her eyes are fixed on her purpose, new energy emerges. Remember, you are forgetting. Paul writes, "I press. I am straining toward, and stretching toward what is ahead, what is before me. I am reaching for what is in front of me, what is in my sight range. I can see my purpose, but it is in front of me and not behind me. It is in my future and not my past. As I press toward it, I am getting closer. The closer I get the less time I have for foolishness. Looking back is not an option now. My focus is on pursuing my destiny and I must press." Just like Apostle Paul, we must press, pursue and not look back to the past.

Press comes from the Greek word *diōkō* (Strong's Concordance G1377) meaning to make to run or flee, put to flight, drive away. Anything that stands between you and God and His purpose for you has to go. *Press* means to run swiftly in order to catch a person or thing, to run after. To press means to run swiftly to reach the goal, also to pursue in a hostile manner. Sometimes we have to get angry with things that stand in our way. Do not let anything stand between you and your purpose. We must be willing to fight when necessary to stay focused on our purpose. The indirect distractions of life are a trick designed to cause believers to abort their destinies. When an individual is serious about accomplishing her destiny, she will not let anybody or anything stand in the way. If you are not walking in the plan of God for your life, stop right now and ask God to forgive you and show you what His plan is for your life. Do not let the enemy offer you a counterfeit. Get furious with the enemy and begin to speak the promises of God over your life. Put satan in his place so you can passionately pursue the call of God for your life.

As I write this, my husband is once again struggling with challenges in his body. About a month ago, he lost the use of his right leg. A magnetic resonance imaging of the thoracic region revealed a tumor in his spinal cord. The doctors told us they were 99 percent sure it was cancer. He had been diagnosed with Hodgkin's lymphoma for the second time in 2008. The first time was in 1977. After undergoing a stem cell transplant in 2009 he has been cancer free.

This new development not only disrupted the plan of God for my husband's life, but it was messing with my destiny as well. We began to pray along with a host of other people and believed God that He would turn the situation around. The options given to my husband by a team of physicians were to have a spinal cord biopsy, which could possibly leave him paralyzed from the chest down. If nothing was done, the cancer would continue to grow, and he eventually would be paralyzed from the chest down. The third option was to treat with radiation since they were sure it was cancer. But this was also dangerous because if the doctors did not know what type of cancer it was, they would not know the appropriate dose of radiation to treat with.

The spinal cord can only take so much radiation, and since he had received radiation in 1977, it was extremely dangerous to give him additional radiation without having all the facts concerning his diagnosis. The spinal cord could be severed, and he was surely to be paralyzed from the chest down. All of the options given to us were not good from my perspective.

The enemy's desire is for you to abandon the plan of God for your life. He comes in all forms to discourage, confuse, depress, and oppress those whom God has called. My husband decided to commit to the biopsy of the spinal cord tumor. After five hours in the operating room, the surgeon came out and declared, "I don't believe it is cancer." This is the same surgeon who told us he was 99 percent sure it was.

In a few days the pathology report came back, and all the doctors were amazed, baffled, and stunned. The report read fibrous tissue. God had turned the situation around. I would not begin to insult the doctor's intelligence. For all we know it could have been cancer, but God had miraculously changed the outcome. You can always know when you are in hot pursuit of God's plan because the enemy will come up against you any way he can. He will use whatever tools, sources, and devices he can to take you off focus. His only goal is to have you not fulfill your God-designed purpose for your life.

As believers we must earnestly endeavor to acquire whatever God has for us. We have to chase after God's plan and God's purpose for our lives. Many times you will need to fight to maintain your focus. We are in spiritual warfare, and one must learn how to fight in the spirit realm. Ephesians 6:12: "For our struggle is not against flesh and blood, but against the rulers, against the authorities, against the powers of this dark world and against the spiritual forces of evil in the heavenly realms."

Our real battle is not with humans but with the demonic beings that work through humans. Continue to pursue God even in the midst of adversity. Things may look challenging, and it may at times look as though you are losing, but remember, if God is for you, who can be against you.

Keep your eye on the prize, even when things are coming against you. Stay focused and be prepared to fight when necessary. Notice I did not say if necessary, but when it is necessary. There will be challenges on this journey to pursue your destiny. No one ever said the call of God for your life would be easy to accomplish.

You may have said, God, I know what you called me to do, but I don't have the provisions. Well can I tell you that God does not give vision without making provisions? The dream that God has given to those who trust Him will always exceed their capabilities to accomplish within themselves. When pursuing the plan of God, financing cannot be our main focus. Who needs resources when we have the source? God is our source.

Women of Promise Ministries Inc. was birthed in my heart several years ago. I hold fast to the promises that God spoke to me then and continues to affirm to me now. I am confident that as I continue to seek God, He will open doors for the ministry to continue.

First Corinthians 2:9: "However, as it is written: 'What no eye has seen, what no ear has heard, and what no human mind has conceived' the things God has prepared for those who love him." The best is yet to come. We have only just begun. God has no respect of persons. (Romans 2:11 KJV). To anyone who has a desire to be used by God, He is able to work in your life. God desires to use us as vessels to promote His cause on the earth. When a believer is hungry for the things of God, that believer can rest in the fact that God will finish what He has started. We have to press on toward the goal, pressing toward our purpose. We were created to be loved by God and to be used by God.

Understanding our purpose goes hand in hand with knowing who we are in Christ. Children of God must know their value. You are a designer's original. God created you unique for His purpose and for His glory.

God has not changed His mind concerning you. Even when it looks dark, stay encouraged. When you feel like crying, continue to praise God. Psalm 22:1-3: "My God, my God, why hast thou forsaken me? why art thou so far from helping me, and from the words of my roaring? O my God, I cry in the day time, but thou hearest not; and in the night season, and am not silent. But thou art holy, O thou that inhabitest the praises of Israel" (KJV).

We are His people, and God inhabits the praises of His people. That word *inhabit* from the Hebrew word *yashab* (Strong's H3427) means to set, to remain, to abode, to dwell. The word *Praise* in this Scripture is *thillah*, (Strong Concordance H8416) which means to praise, adoration, thanksgiving (paid to God) act of general or public praise, praise-song (as title) praise (demanded by qualities or deeds or attributes of God) renown, fame, glory of Damascus, God object of praise, possessor of renown.

The Hebrew word for praise in Psalm 150:6, "Let everything that has breath praise the Lord. Praise the Lord" (Strong's Concordance H1984), is *halal* which means to shine (fig. of God's favour), to flash forth light, to praise, boast, to be boastful, to be praised, be made praiseworthy, be commended, be worthy of praise, to make a fool of, make into a fool, to act madly, act like a madman. Praise is not done with caution, quietly, or conservatively. True praise is when a person loses sight of who is around and doesn't mind giving God the praise due Him. We offer adoration and thanksgiving to the One who has called us to serve in His kingdom.

If you want to know the plan of God for your life, then you begin to praise Him in spite of your situation. You begin to give Him glory regardless of what you are going through. Praise gets God's attention. Complaining is not the key that opens the door to God's miracles, but praise will cause God to move on your behalf.

God had a plan for you before He created you. As you seek Him, the plan of God will be revealed to you. There must be a deep hunger and thirst for God and for His plan. If one truly desires to walk in the plan of God, there must be quality, intimate time spent with

God. It is not enough to pray at night before going to bed. The prayer life of an individual who is seeking to walk in the plan of God must be expanded beyond the norm.

As you passionately pursue God and His plan for your life, know that He is faithful to answer when you call. Begin preparing yourself through prayer, wise counsel, and education as you pursue God like never before. Let God know that you are serious about walking out your destiny, but remain obedient to the Word of God and to those He has given charge over you.

As you walk in the plan and purpose of God for your life, you will see submission is very important. Learn to listen to wise counsel. You do not want to get ahead of God, and you do not want to linger too far behind. Pursue Him, and He will manifest Himself to you as never before.

Closing Prayer from the Author

Dear Heavenly Father

I thank You, first of all, for the privilege You have given me to speak into the lives of Your women all over the world through the pages of this book. I pray for every woman who reads this book. I pray that You will grant her clarity of the call You have for her life. Let her know without a doubt that she has been called by You for such a time as this. Empower her now with Your Holy Spirit so that she will move out in faith, focusing on what You have called her to do. I pray against any obstacle that stands between her and her doing what You have called her to do. Help her to realize that You have not given her the spirit of fear but of power and love. "For the Spirit God gave us does not make us timid, but gives us power, love and self-discipline" (2 Timothy 1:7).

Help her to understand that no weapon that is formed against her will prosper. "'No weapon forged against you will prevail, and you will refute every tongue that accuses you. This is the heritage of the servants of the Lord, and this is their vindication from me,' declares the Lord" (Isaiah 54:17). Help her to rest in You, knowing that what You have called her to do will be accomplished through You as she trusts and obeys Your Word. As she moves out in faith, teach her not to lean on her own understanding but to trust You. "Trust in the Lord with all your heart and lean not on your own understanding; in all your ways submit to him, and he will make your paths straight" (Proverbs 3:5-6). Let her know that You are her source, and that all power comes from You.

Lord, I pray that she would not grow weary in well doing but will be encouraged by Your Word and by others to keep moving forward. "Let us not become weary in doing good, for at the proper time we will reap a harvest if we do not give up" (Galatians 6:9). Even when the storms come, help her to hold on to Your hand. I pray that she will not be influenced by the fame or glamour that so many seek after in ministry. Help her to understand that the call is to accomplish Your purpose. I thank You, Lord Jesus, for those who, after reading this book, will be motivated to pursue what You have called them to do. I pray that the words of this book with the words from the Word of God will strengthen them and position them to walk in the call that you have for their lives. Let them press toward the mark of the higher calling, not looking back. "Brothers and sisters, I do not consider myself yet to have taken hold of it. But one thing I do: Forgetting what is behind and straining toward what is ahead, I press on toward the goal to win the prize for which God has called me heavenward in Christ Jesus" (Philippians 3:13-14).

Lord, I thank You for being faithful to use me in ministry for many years, and I still feel the urgency and excitement that I felt many years ago when You first called me. As You continue to open doors in my life, I commit myself to be obedient to what You have called me to do.

Thank You for the privilege to serve You as a single woman, then as a wife and mother. Thank You for the opportunity to serve in ministry as a servant first and to be able to share the good news of the Gospel to so many people. You have blessed me to be an entrepreneur as a writer, and for that I am grateful. It is through the many doors that You have opened that I am able to touch the lives of people. I take no credit for what has been accomplished through my life; all of the honor and glory goes to You. Thank You, thank You, this I pray In Jesus' name. Amen.

Partial List of Women in the Bible

Mary	Rebekah
Ruth	Huldah
Rachel	Elisabeth
Miriam	Esther
Martha	Eunice
Dinah	Eve
Dorcas	Gomer
Abigail	Delilah
Hagar	Elisabeth
Anna	Jecholiah
Jedidah	Joanna
Jochebed	Jemima
Judith	Junia
Jezebel	Lois
Lydia	Martha
Mary Magdalene	Milcah
Naomi	Orpah
Phoebe	Priscilla
Rahab	Rebekah
Rhoda	Leah
Sapphira	Sarah
Tamar	Vashti
Zeresh	Zilpah

Zipporah   Priscilla
Bathsheba   Hannah
Jezebel   Deborah

This is a partial list of women who are mentioned in Scripture. It is my prayer that you will do your own personal research to see what part these and other women had in Bible history and in the ministry of Jesus. As you read about women in the Bible, it will encourage you and help you to understand that you have a place in Scripture and that God is still using women today to accomplish His purpose on the earth.

Additional Resources

Barclay, William. Commentaries of the New Testament. Philadelphia, Westminster John Knox Press 2004.

Earle, Ralph. Word Meaning in the New Testament. Kansas City, Missouri. Beacon Hill Press of Kansas City. 1986.

Henry, Matthew. Romans chapter 16. Matthew Henry Commentary on the Whole Bible (Complete). Bible Study Tools Online. Web. 11 Mar. 2013.

Strong, James. The New Strong's Exhaustive Concordance of the Bible. Nashville, Tennessee Thomas Nelson Inc., 1990.

Strong's Concordance with Hebrew and Greek Lexicon." Strong's Concordance with Hebrew and Greek Lexicon. King James Version, n.d. Web. 02 Jan. 2012.

The Nelson Study Bible. Earl D. Radmacher, Th.D., general editor. Nashville, Tennessee: Thomas Nelson Publisher, 1997.

Vine, W. E. Vine's Complete Expository Dictionary of Old and New Testament Words. Nashville, Tennessee: Thomas Nelson Inc., 1996.

About the Author

D r. Evelyn Johnson-Taylor was called by God to minister to women. The call of God has not been without challenges, but she has dedicated her life to encouraging and teaching women from all walks of life. Her heart is for the spiritual growth and development of women. She is the founder of Women of Promise Ministries Inc. and Evelyn J Taylor Ministries.

> Evelyn worked as a registered nurse in critical care for twelve years and as a Realtor for five years prior to pursuing her calling as a full time women's ministry leader. After being called by God to minster to women, she sought to further

prepare herself through education. She has earned a bachelor's degree in women's studies, and a master's and Ph.D. in ministry

Dr. Johnson-Taylor is also a published author who speaks, teaches, and preaches about women's issues. Her book titles include *Women of Promise, Seven Blessing Blockers*, and *Identity Crisis*.

She is married to Pastor Scott B. Taylor, and they are the blessed parents of two daughters.

Women of Promise Ministries Inc

Women of Promise Ministries Inc. is a 501 (c) (3) outreach ministry founded by Dr. Evelyn Johnson-Taylor. This ministry assists those in need, both spiritually and physically, by providing mentoring, teaching, training, and coaching.

Mission Statement:

Our mission is to encourage women to seek a deeper relationship with Jesus Christ.

Purpose:

We want women to develop a Hunger and to discover every promise God has made in His Word. After discovering God's promises, women will be empowered, not only to possess the promises, but to share and encourage other women to receive the promises of God.

Our purpose is to assist in nurturing and developing the gifts that God has given each of us. It is our desire to see women whole and actively pursuing their destiny. Women of Promise Ministries provides an opportunity for women to communicate and encourage one another via e-mail, telephone, and personal contact.

Goal and Vision:

To reach women all over the world from all walks of life.

To provide training, mentoring, coaching, and teaching by having an annual Women of Promise conference.

To offer workshops and seminars throughout the year.

To establish local Women of Promise Ministries that meet monthly in various parts of the world. This time will be used to discuss issues that are relevant to women and to provide a biblical perspective.

What We Believe:

All Scripture is inspired by God.

There is only one God and the only way to Him is by receiving Jesus Christ as your personal Savior and Lord.

Salvation is by grace through faith and not of works.

Christ will return. He has prepared a place for
those who have received Him to dwell with Him
in eternity (2 Timothy 3:16; John 14:6; Ephesians
2:8; John 14:3; 1 Thessalonians 4:16-17).

Quite often we want to possess the promises
without meeting the conditions. It is our desire that
women will have a hunger to know God. Not an
intellectual "know" but an intimate "know." Apostle
Paul writes in Philippians 3:10, "I want to know Christ
and the power of his resurrection and the fellowship
of sharing in his sufferings, becoming like him in his
death." Many times we ask, "If God loves me, why did
this happen to me?" The question is not if God loves
us. The question is "Do we love Him? Do we love Him
enough to obey His Word? Do we love Him enough to
really seek to 'know' Him?" Ask yourself the question
"How much do I love God?" It is our sincere prayer
that you will love God with all of your heart and seek
to know Him intimately. Dr. Johnson-Taylor's mandate
from God is to teach women how to walk in obedience
to His Word. It is vital that we allow the Holy Spirit
to guide us toward our purpose so that we can become
true women of promise.

CPSIA information can be obtained at www.ICGtesting.com
Printed in the USA
LVOW10s1140061215

465619LV00023B/2430/P